Educational Facilities

1995-96 Review

First published in the United States of America by
Rockport Publishers, Inc.
146 Granite Street
Rockport, Massachusetts 01966-1299
Telephone 508 546 9590
Fax 508 546 7141

Distributed to the book trade and art trade by
The AIA Press
1735 New York Avenue
Washington, D.C. 20006
Telephone 800 365 2724
Fax 802 864 7626

Other distribution by
Rockport Publishers
Rockport, Massachusetts

ISBN 1-55835-142-6

10 9 8 7 6 5 4 3 2 1

American Institute of Architects
Committee on Architecture for Education
Advisory Group 1995-96

William "Sandy" Stevenson, AIA, *1996 Chair*
Gaylaird Christopher, AIA, *1995 Chair*
W. Jeff Floyd, FAIA, *Vice Chair*
Richard J. Passantino, AIA
James T. Biehle, AIA
Steve Crane, AIA

American Institute of Architects Staff

David Roccosalva, *Director*, Educational Facilities
Glennette Clark, *Coordinator*, Information Management
Jane Opera, *Past Coordinator*, Information Management

DESIGN: Group C, Inc.
LAYOUT: Jennie Bush, Books By Design, Inc.
PAGING: Carol Keller
COVER PHOTOGRAPH: Timothy Hursley *(project appears on page 24)*

Manufactured in China
by Regent Publishing Services Limited

Educational Facilities

1995-96 Review

The American Institute of Architects Press

Washington, D.C.

Contents

1996 Jury

CARL B. BOYINGTON is the administrative director of facilities for the Weber School District, Ogden, Utah. He is responsible for all new construction and school remodeling, land sales and acquisition, and maintenance and operation of all facilities in a school district with ongoing new construction. Boyington has thirty years experience as a teacher and school principal.

CHARLES W. JONES III, AIA, is a principal and the director of design for the Architectural Design Group in Oklahoma City. He has twelve years of experience on a wide range of projects, including numerous public schools, a child development center, and several college and university facilities. Jones is a member of the AIA Committee on Architecture for Education and an associate member of the Cooperative Council of School Administrators in Oklahoma.

ROGER F. NEWILL, AIA, is a principal in the firm Hanbury Evans Newill Vlattas & Company, Norfolk, Virginia. He has designed and prepared plans for a number of colleges and universities in Virginia, including a dorm itory and dining facilities master plan for Virginia Polytechnic Institute and State University in Blacksburg, a campus master plan for Longwood College in Farmville, a master plan for Old Dominion University, housing plans for George Mason University in Fairfax, and a cultural arts facility for the Virginia Military Institute in Lexington.

KATHERINE N. RUSS, AIA, is a principal in the firm of Boney Architects, a nationally recognized leader in the field of educational facility design. Boney Architects was founded in 1922 in Wilmington, North Carolina, and has expanded in recent years to include offices in Raleigh and Charlotte, North Carolina. Russ joined the firm in 1988 and was named director of the Raleigh office in 1992. As project architect for more than twenty new school projects throughout North Carolina, she has established her expertise in educational facility design. Russ is a member of the AIA Committee on Architecture for Education and the Council of Educational Facility Planners International.

ELTON "DALE" SCHEIDEMAN, AIA, is the director of facilities planning for the Clark County, Nevada, School District. He helped complete a $675 million bond capital improvement program, constructing fifty-seven new schools in seven years. He was also responsible for formulating the building program and budget for a $605 million bond fund, which will provide twenty-five new schools and rehabilitate and modernize 114 older schools over a five-year period. Scheideman has more than forty years experience in planning, design, construction, maintenance, and management of government and institutional facilities. He has directed planning and design consultants on a broad range of master planning, building design, environmental, and construction programs in the United States and abroad.

Jury Statement

The 40 projects featured in this volume present state-of-the-practice projects in educational facilities design. This collection is the result of the first American Institute of Architects Commitee on Architecture for Education competition to identify projects of such caliber.

All of the projects the jury reviewed carry out their traditional functions well, but the jury was looking for projects that also respond to new departures in educational programming and administration.

Several questions posed by the jury face all communities, and consideration of these is vital for architects working in this discipline area. For example, how can the "towns and villages" of teaching be accurately defined: by age group, by discipline, or by another model such as the house concept? How can the downtown/suburban split in school-age population be avoided?

A few trends worth noting were revealed in the projects included here: They offer a refreshing variety of approaches to the corridor/classroom approach, from multidisciplinary "houses" along a central "Main Street" to a school that itself functions as an indoor/outdoor classroom in the desert. The designs of many projects featured here have paid close attention to faculty and administrative spaces, recognizing and affirming the professional status of educators. Two entries in childhood development represent the wave of the future, as day care facilities for children become more central and multipurpose in their parents' daily lives. There were surprisingly few university submissions; time will tell whether this indicates a larger trend in the design and development of such facilities.

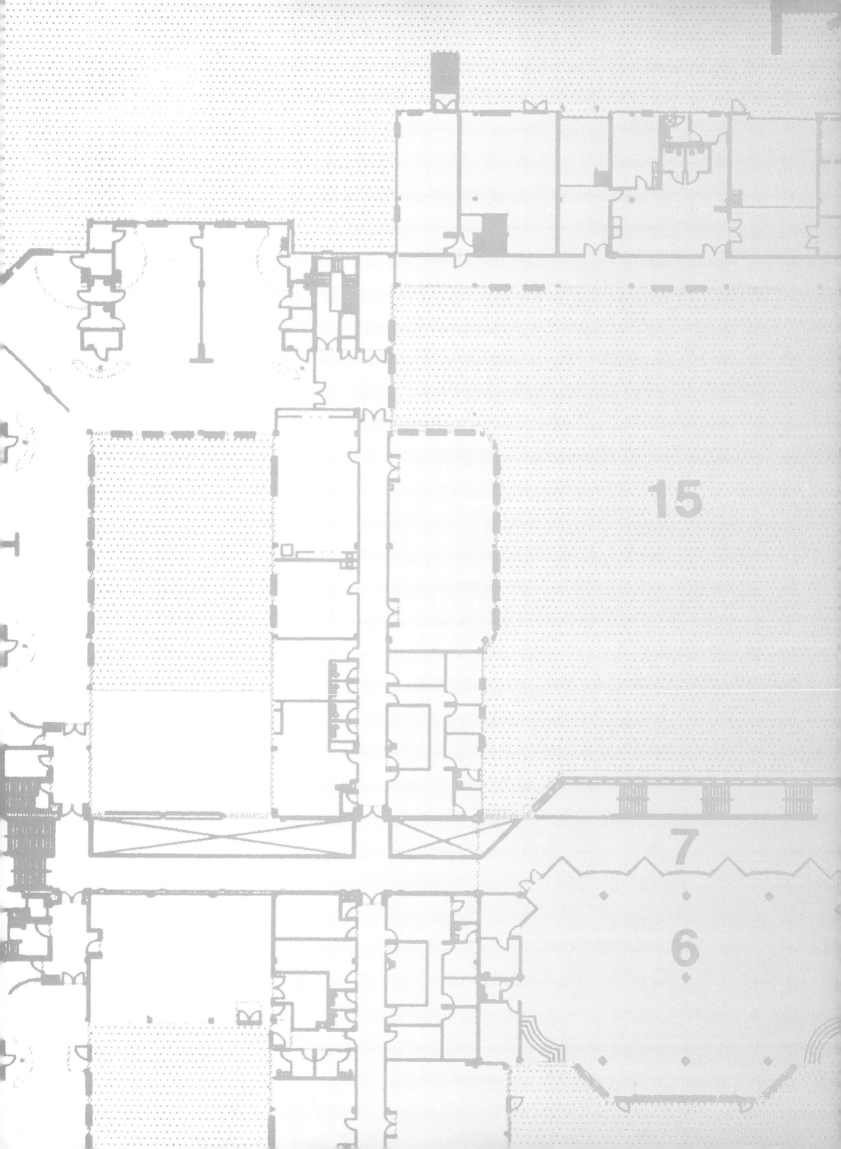

Childhood Development Centers

Stanley M. Makowski Early Childhood Center

Buffalo, New York

Citation

The Stanley M. Makowski Early Childhood Center reflects the future, as day care for young children takes on increased importance. While this is an early childhood center, the building is well-integrated into the community it serves, providing a wellness program, health care facilities, and community outreach focused on parenting skills.

Each of the six play areas in this large, urban public day care center is for a different age group and reflects a different theme related to nature and science. Although the building serves a large number of children (2,000 students) and their parents, the scale and detailing help it relate well to the children with a softness and looseness that makes it comfortable without being "cute."

Owner
Buffalo Board of Education

Data
Type of Facility
Early childhood center

Type of Construction
New

Area of Building
176,130 GSF

Area of Courtyards
39,300 GSF

Cost of Construction
$20,400,000

Cost of Educational Equipment
$2,500,000

Status of Project
Completed January 1995

Credits
Architect
Foit-Albert Associates, Architecture,
Engineering and Surveying, P.C.
763 Main Street
Buffalo, New York 14203

*Educational Programming and
Consulting Architect*
Passantino & Bavier, Inc.,
a subsidiary of the Facilities Group
2401 Lake Park Drive, Suite 250
Smyrna, Georgia 30080

*Structural/Mechanical/Electrical
Engineer*
C & S Engineers, Inc.
Buffalo, New York

Landscape Architect
Peter J. Smith & Co., Inc.
Buffalo, New York

Construction Manager
Cannon Program Management
Grand Island, New York

Photographer
David Gordon
Buffalo, New York

ARCHITECT'S STATEMENT

A comprehensive early childhood development program requires multiple services that have traditionally been scattered throughout the community. Faced with a large student population and extensive community functions, a scale appropriate for young children was achieved by dividing the school into a community "house" and three academic "houses" arranged along an atrium "Main Street" that provides a central focus for the school and community. Each academic house has classrooms, offices, a dining area, and a playcourt. The houses also share two large playcourts: one for large muscle play, and one for outdoor science instruction. For program flexibility, the fourth wall of each classroom is open to shared commons rooms and can be closed off or opened up with movable furniture.

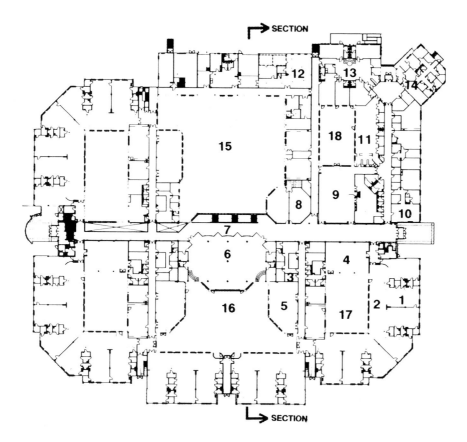

SECTION

KEY

1 Classroom
2 Commons
3 House Admin.
4 Fitness Room
5 Dining
6 Library
7 Atrium
8 Computer
9 Multi-Purpose
10 Administration
11 Latchkey
12 Kitchen
13 Daycare
14 Well-Baby Clinic
15 Activity
   Courtyard
16 Science &
   Nature
   Courtyard
17 Typ. Courtyard
18 Latchkey
   Courtyard

SECTION

**Second
Level
Plan**

0   30   60

Childhood Development Centers

Early Childhood Development Center
University of Notre Dame

Notre Dame, Indiana

ARCHITECT'S STATEMENT

The Early Childhood Development Center is established to serve the faculty, staff and students of the university. The facility is licensed to serve 165 two-to six-year olds, as well as school age children during summer months. The Center was designed to establish a sense of place, fascination, and playful instruction, yet blend well with the university environment. The exterior is designed using much of the architectural vocabulary prevalent on the campus, but assembles the pieces in a more playful manner. The building is composed of the standard "university brick" but also sports a blue roof and green trim to remain collegiate and kindergarten at the same time. Geometric design elements are the theme of the structure and are repeated throughout the building. Skylights bring an abundance of daylight into the main corridor of the building and expansive windows provide views of the 1.6-acre wooded lot. A central gathering area, designated by architectural detail which repeats the geometric theme, is used for presenters such as storytellers and puppeteers.

Owner
University of Notre Dame

Data

Type of Facility
Early childhood center

Type of Construction
New

Area of Building
12,800 GSF

Cost of Construction
$1,400,000

Status of Project
Completed August 1994

Credits

Architect
The Trover Group, Inc.
415 Lincolnway East
Mishawaka, Indiana 46544

*Structural/Mechanical/Electrical
Engineer*
The Trover Group, Inc.
Mishawaka, Indiana

Contractor
Casteel Construction Corporation
South Bend, Indiana

Photographer
Bruce Harlan
South Bend, Indiana

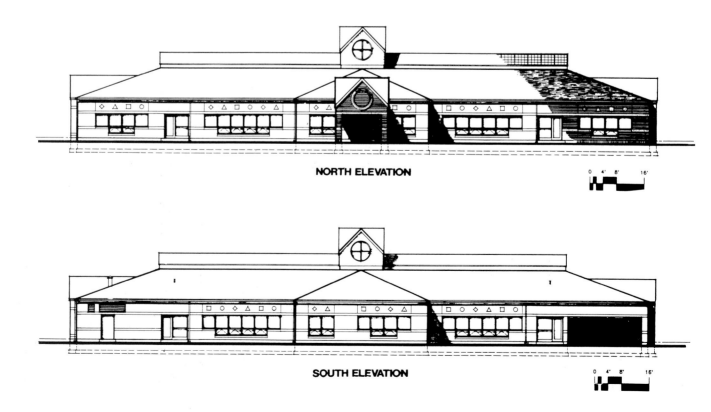

NORTH ELEVATION

0 4' 8' 16'

SOUTH ELEVATION

0 4' 8' 16'

Childhood Development Centers

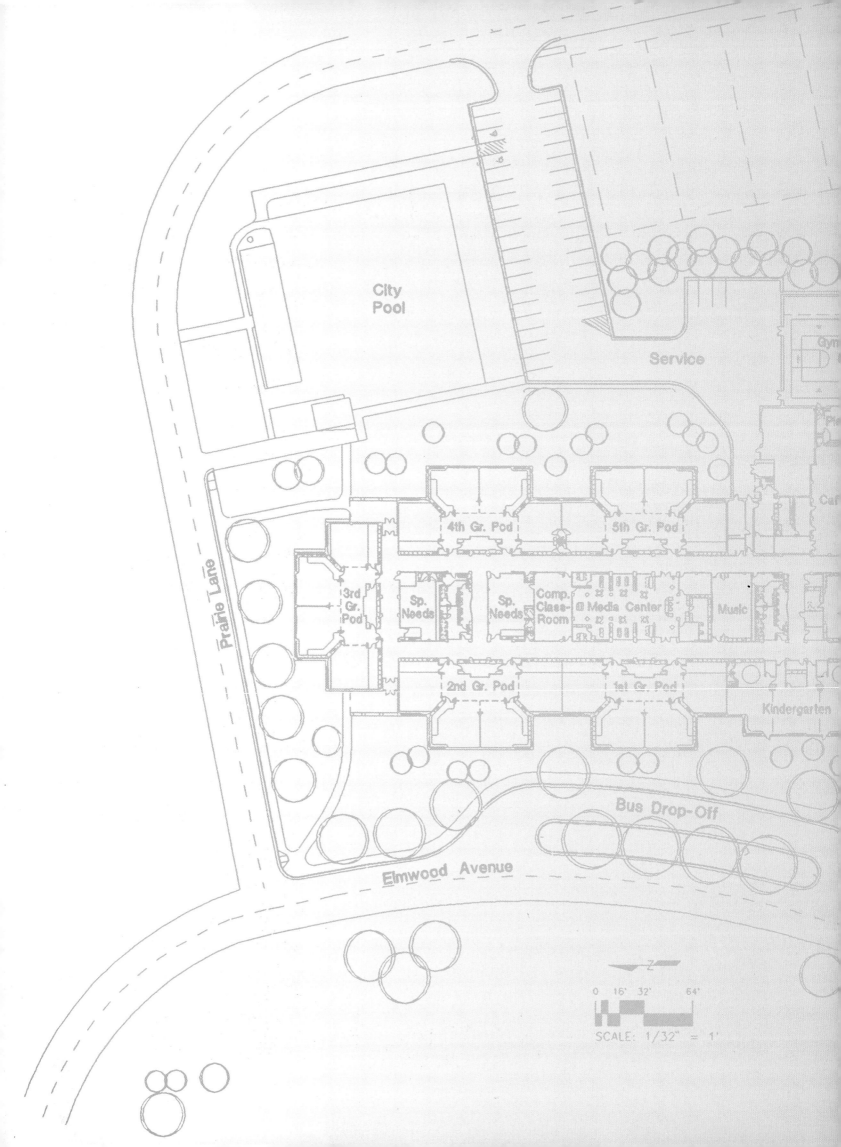

Elementary Schools

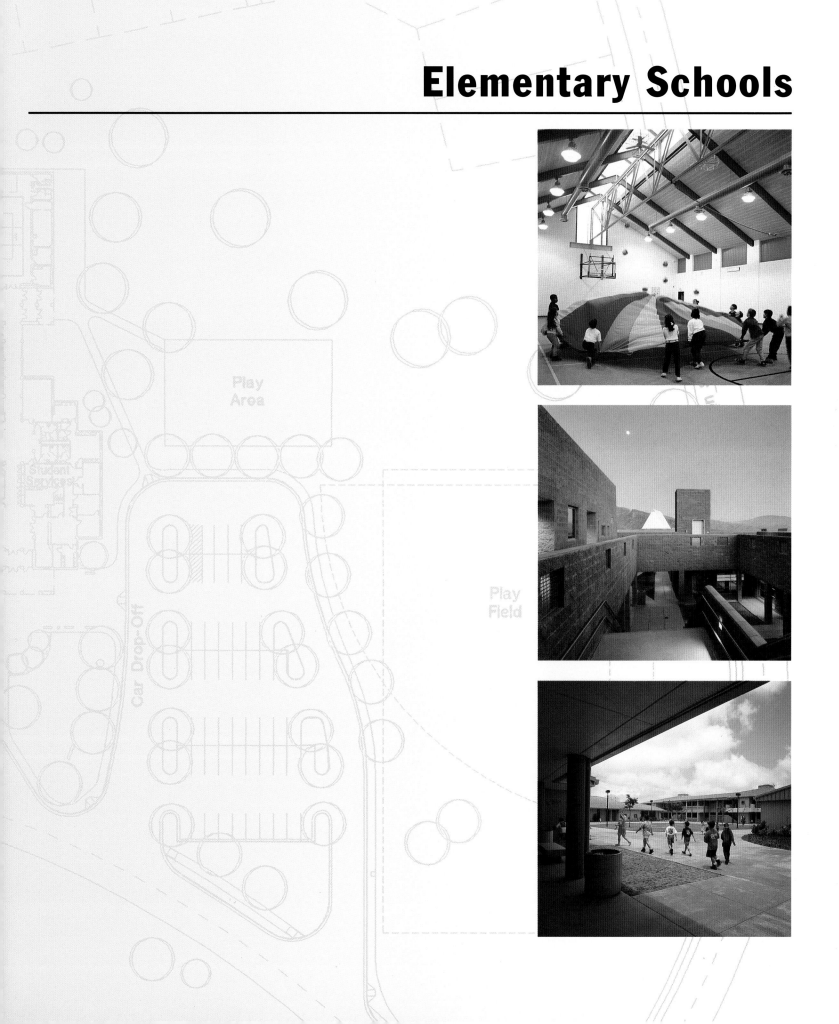

Play
Area

Student
Services

Car Drop-Off

Play
Field

Roberto Clemente Elementary School #8

Rochester, New York

Citation

The plan is impressively simple for this urban elementary school for 800 students from preschool through the fifth grade. It responds well to its sloping site, with changes in elevation, massing, and finish that allow its integration into a residential neighborhood. It provides a media center, a unique clinic with space for doctors to treat children on site, and two adult classrooms for continuing education.

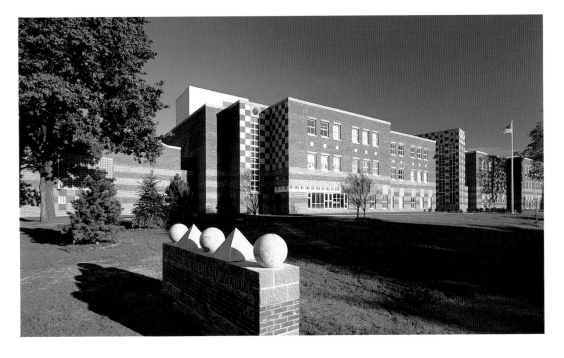

Owner
Rochester City School District

Data
Type of Facility
Elementary school

Type of Construction
New

Area of Building
96,654 GSF

Cost of Construction
$9,300,000

Status of Project
Completed September 1994

Credits
Architect
Cannon
2170 Whitehaven Road
Grand Island, New York 14072

*Structural / Mechanical / Electrical
Engineer*
Cannon
Grand Island, New York

Contractor
Christa Construction
Victor, New York

Photographers
Tim Wilkes (Building)
Rochester, New York

James Cavanaugh (Model)
North Tonawanda, New York

ARCHITECT'S STATEMENT

This inner-city elementary school was commissioned to replace a 100-year-old facility–the district's oldest. With an anticipated life of more than 50 years, the building is designed to retain the scale, intimacy, and security of smaller neighborhood schools, yet accommodate a growing student body of 800, as well as service-changing educational and community needs in the future. The three-story structure is distinguished by the colorful interplay of geometric shapes and forms on its exterior, which announce it as a place for children to learn and grow.

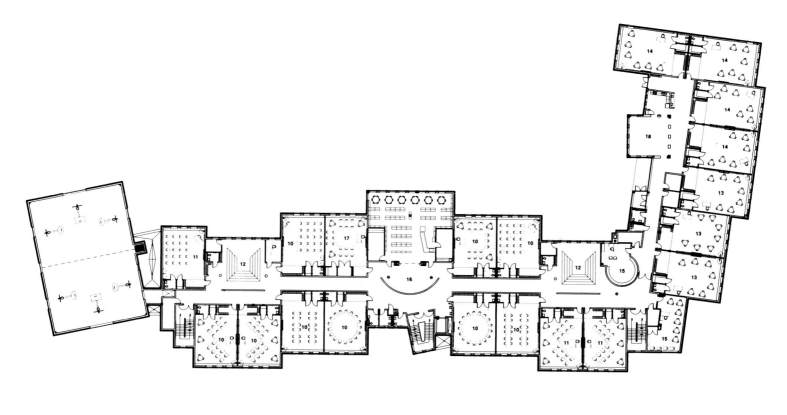

10. CLASSROOM
11. SPECIAL EDUCATION CLASSROOM
12. OPEN CLASSROOM AREA
13. KINDERGARTEN CLASSROOM
14. PRE-K CLASSROOM
15. RESOURCE ROOM
16. LIBRARY
17. COMPUTER ROOM
18. COMMON AREA

LEVEL 2

Scale
0   16   32   64

N

Elementary Schools

Ventana Vista Elementary School

Tucson, Arizona

Citation

This elementary school is unique in the fact that it is itself a teaching tool. Sited in the desert, it responds strongly to its locale and topography with use of iconographic forms, pattern, texture, light and shadow, and color. Its challenging forms and spaces make no gesture to coziness: instead, the building as a whole creates an educational setting in which a variety of "unassigned" areas become laboratories for learning. The major landmark for the entire school is the tent over the multipurpose room. It acts as a shading device for skylights but also connects the school to its origins of ancient desert nomadic encampments.

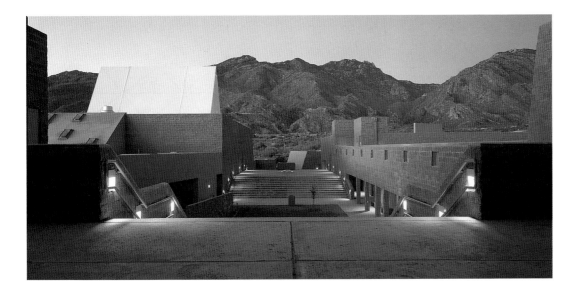

Owner
Catalina Foothills School District

Data
Type of Facility
Elementary school

Type of Construction
New

Area of Building
90,000 GSF

Cost of Construction
$6,784,678

Cost of Educational Equipment
$1,603,658

Status of Project
Completed August 1994

Credits
Design Architect
Antoine Predock
300 12th Street, N.W.
Albuquerque, New Mexico 87102

Architect of Record
Burns-Wald-Hopkins Architects
2940 North Swan Road, #214
Tucson, Arizona 85712

Structural Engineer
Turner Structural Engineers
Tucson, Arizona

Mechanical Engineer
Adams and Associates
Tucson, Arizona

Electrical Engineer
Monrad Engineering
Tucson, Arizona

Civil Engineer
McGovern, MacVittie, Lodge and
Associates
Tucson, Arizona

Landscape Architect
Acuna-Coffeen Landscape
Architects
Tucson, Arizona

(credits continue)

ARCHITECT'S STATEMENT

Ventana Vista Elementary School is located in a fragile desert ecosystem at the base of the Catalina Mountains. Approaching the site, vehicles remain above the arroyo cutting across the site. Across the wash, one enters the realm of children. Each age group of students occupies its respective village. Each village has its own landmark to guide the children through the site. At the major crossroads of the villages are the common spaces: the library and the multi-purpose room.

Opportunities for outdoor assembly are provided throughout the children's city. Each village has its own court with seating and experiment areas. Ventana Vista encourages exploration of the desert environment and a journey through a children's city of imagination and memory.

Credits (continued)
Furnishings Consultant
   Interior Technology Associates
   Tucson, Arizona

Contractor
   Diversified Design & Construction
   Tucson, Arizona

Photographer
   Timothy Hursley
   Little Rock, Arkansas

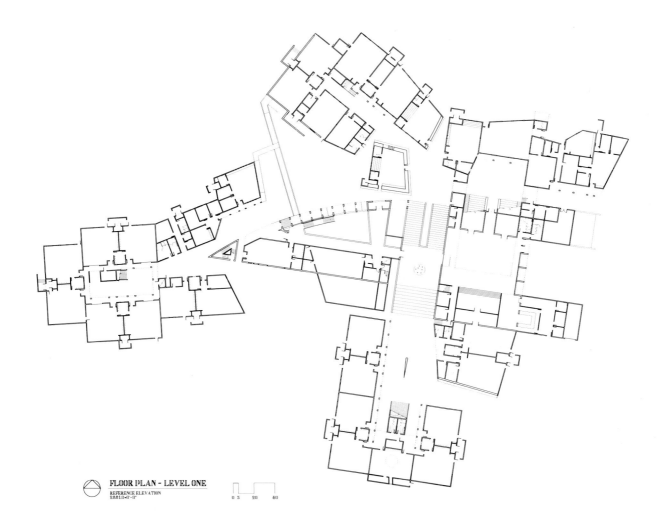

FLOOR PLAN - LEVEL ONE
REFERENCE ELEVATION
2881.0'-0'-0"

0 5   20   40

Amelia Elementary School

Amelia, Virginia

ARCHITECT'S STATEMENT

The project is an example of the school-within-a-school concept that connects two distinct academic "houses" to a central "Main Street." Isolating the K-2 classrooms and children from the upper elementary classrooms precludes the need for students in one area to enter the other (thereby improving supervision and decreasing the potential for interruption of in-progress instruction), and locates each group of students as closely as possible to core academic areas.

The project was designed to accommodate the projected elementary grade level population of the entire county, to provide the infrastructure for current and future state-of-the-art educational technology, and to reflect the architectural character of the surrounding rural community.

Owner
Amelia County Public Schools

Data

Type of Facility
Elementary school

Type of Construction
New

Area of Building
87,280 GSF

Cost of Construction
$5,827,198

Status of Project
Completed September 1993

Credits

Architect
Bond Comet Westmoreland + Hiner
Architects
207 West Broad Street
Richmond, Virginia 23220

Structural Engineer
Hanover Engineers
Richmond, Virginia

Mechanical/Electrical Engineer
Simmons Rockecharlie & Prince
Richmond, Virginia

Civil Engineer
Austin Brochenbrough &
Associates
Chester, Virginia

(credits continue)

Credits (continued)
Landscape Architect
Higgins & Associates
Richmond, Virginia

Contractor
C.L. Lewis & Co., Inc.
Lynchburg, Virginia

Photographer
James Adcock
Richmond, Virginia

Elementary Schools   30

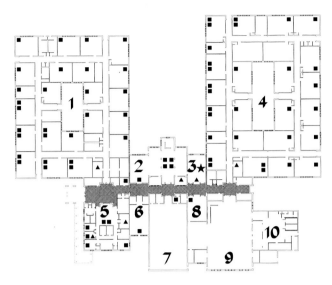

PLAN:

1 Academic Neighborhood (Grades 3-5)
2 Media Center
3 Computer Lab
4 Academic Neighborhood (Grades K-2)
5 Administration
6 Art
7 Gymnasium
8 Music
9 Cafetorium
10 Kitchen
Main Street

TECHNOLOGY LEGEND:

■ **PC**
486SX-33, 4MB RAM, 130 MB Hard
Drive, Sound Blaster, Pro Soundcard,
Headphones, Speakers, Network Card

▲ **FILE SERVER/CD ROM FILE SERVER**
486DX-66, 8MB RAM, 341 MB Hard
Drive, SCSI CD ROM Drives

★ **COMPUTER LABORATORY**
26 Workstations, CCC Laboratory w/ 10
Workstations

NETWORK SOFTWARE: LANTASTIC

Coyote Canyon Elementary School

Rancho Cucamonga, California

ARCHITECT'S STATEMENT

Four theme courtyards have been incorporated into the design to bring early history to life. The courtyards represent major periods in the history of the city. The first courtyard is the Native American Courtyard. Next is the Spanish/Mexican Courtyard, which the second and third grades will look out onto. A third courtyard represents the mission. The fourth courtyard will remind the students of the State of California's first vineyards. It is hoped that the school's historical setting will become a community element that will benefit residents beyond the students attending the school.

Owner
Central School District

Data

Type of Facility
Elementary school

Type of Construction
New

Area of Building
49,000 GSF

Cost of Construction
$5,900,000

Status of Project
Completed April 1992

Credits

Architect
Wolff/Lang/Christopher Architects
10470 Foothill Boulevard,
Tower Suite
Rancho Cucamonga, California
91730

Structural Engineer
K.B. Leung and Associates, Inc.
Alta Loma, California

Mechanical Engineer
F.T. Andrews, Inc.
Anaheim, California

Electrical Engineer
RWR Pascoe Engineering, Inc.
Irvine, California

Civil Engineer
KWC Engineers, Inc.
Corona, California

Energy Consultant
Energy Strategy, Inc.
Sacramento, California

Kitchen Consultant
Commercial Kitchen Design
La Canada-Flintridge, California

Landscape Architect
RHA Landscape Architects,
Planners, Inc.
Riverside, California

Contractor
Tilden-Coil Constructors
Riverside, California

Photographer
Fred Daly
Chino Hills, California

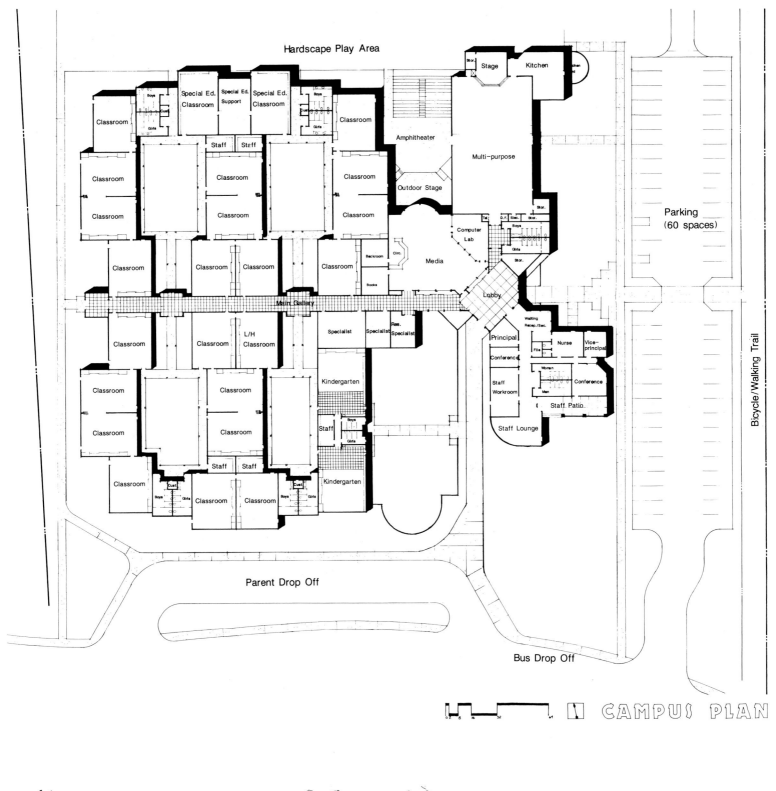

Hardscape Play Area

Classroom

Special Ed. Classroom

Special Ed. Support

Special Ed. Classroom

Boys

Girls

Classroom

Stage

Kitchen

Staff

Staff

Classroom

Classroom

Classroom

Amphitheater

Multi-purpose

Classroom

Classroom

Classroom

Outdoor Stage

Tel. D.F. Elec. Stor.

Boys

Stor.

Classroom

Classroom

Classroom

Classroom

Backroom

Circ.

Computer Lab

Girls

Stor.

Books

Media

Stor.

Lobby

Parking
(60 spaces)

Main Gallery

Classroom

Classroom

L/H Classroom

Classroom

Specialist

Specialist

Res. Specialist

Principal

Waiting Recep./Sec.

Nurse

Vice-principal

Conference

File

Women

Conference

Classroom

Classroom

Classroom

Kindergarten

Staff Workroom

Men

Classroom

Classroom

Staff

Boys

Girls

Staff Patio

Staff Lounge

Staff

Staff

Kindergarten

Classroom

Cust

Classroom

Classroom

Cust

Boys

Girls

Boys

Girls

Bicycle/Walking Trail

Parent Drop Off

Bus Drop Off

CAMPUS PLAN

WEST ELEVATION

35 Elementary Schools

Discovery Elementary School

Brigham City, Utah

ARCHITECT'S STATEMENT

The school was designed to fit the small scale of the site, as well as the scale and colors of the neighborhood. Life in the community is dominated by two sources of income: farming, and work in the nearby space shuttle manufacturing plant. The school was named for the space shuttle. Farming is recognized by the school's entrance canopies. Just as the countryside is dotted with canopies covering haystacks for protection from the harsh elements, the entry canopies protect children from the same harsh weather.

Sloping metal roofs reflect many of the surrounding buildings common throughout the area. The school's materials and colors are indicative of the area.

Owner
   Box Elder School District

Data
   Type of Facility
   Elementary school

   Type of Construction
   New

   Area of Building
   42,673 GSF

   Cost of Construction
   $3,036,616

   Cost of Educational Equipment
   $350,000

   Status of Project
   Completed September 1994

Credits
   Architect
   Valentiner Crane Brunjes Onyon
   Architects, P.C.
   524 South 600 East
   Salt Lake City, Utah 84102

   Structural Engineer
   Craig Cartwright
   Logan, Utah

(credits continue)

Credits (continued)

Mechanical Engineer
Bennion Associates
Salt Lake City, Utah

Electrical Engineer
BNA Consulting Engineers
Salt Lake City, Utah

Landscape Architect
Jim Webster
Salt Lake City, Utah

Contractor
Union Pointe Construction
Salt Lake City, Utah

Photographer
Scot Zimmerman
Park City, Utah

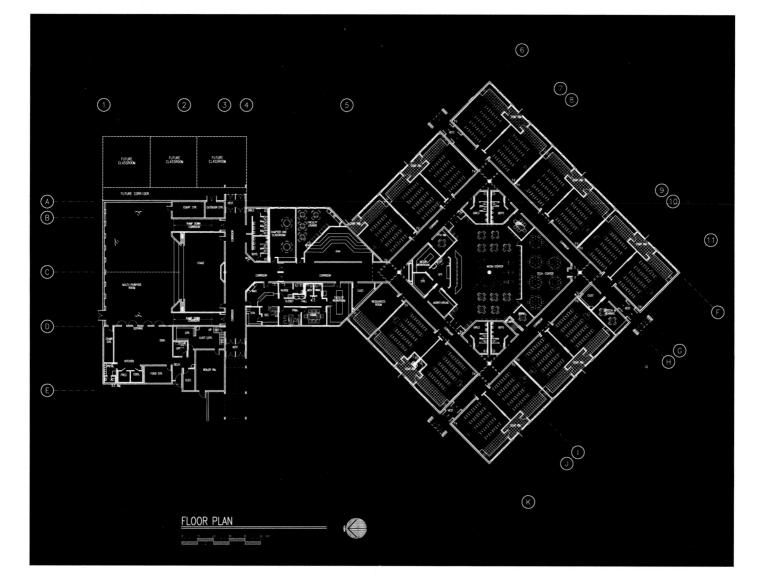

FLOOR PLAN

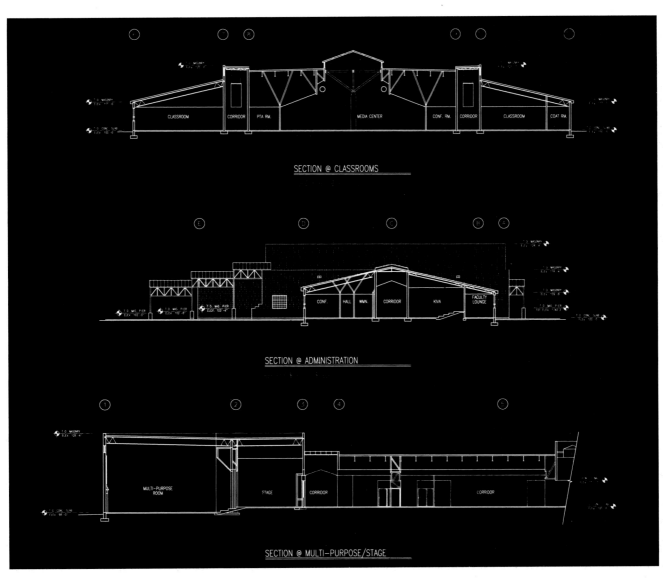

SECTION @ CLASSROOMS

SECTION @ ADMINISTRATION

SECTION @ MULTI-PURPOSE/STAGE

Mililani Mauka Elementary School

Mililani, Hawaii

ARCHITECT'S STATEMENT

This prototype school integrates current and future educational technology while emphasizing a home-like environment. Also serving as a community center for educational, cultural and recreational events, it features four simple residential-scale buildings. Local earth-tone stucco and colored textured concrete block walls, together with tinted window glass and sloping roofs, respond to the tropical climate, harmonizing with the natural environment and surrounding community.

Interior spaces are tailored to a child's scale and grouped into color-coded clusters to provide children with a more intimate sense of belonging. Museum-like neutral finishes offer opportunities for children and teachers to create their own special environments.

Owner
   Central District, Department of
   Education State of Hawaii

Data
   Type of Facility
   Elementary school

   Type of Construction
   New

   Area of Building
   91,500 GSF

   Cost of Construction
   $13,000,000

   Cost of Educational Equipment
   $600,000

   Status of Project
   Completed August 1995

Credits
   Architect
      Peter Hsi Associates, Inc.
      615 Piikoi Street, Suite 2001
      Honolulu, Hawaii 96814

   Structural Engineer
      Engineering Design Group, Inc.
      Honolulu, Hawaii

   Mechanical Engineer
      Charles T. Lunson & Associates
      Honolulu, Hawaii

   Electrical Engineer
      Bennett Engineers, Inc.
      Honolulu, Hawaii

   Civil Engineer
      Hida, Okamoto & Associates
      Honolulu, Hawaii

   Information Technology Consultant
      Robin Consulting International
      Honolulu, Hawaii

   Contractor
      Tower Construction, Inc., General
      Contractors
      Honolulu, Hawaii

   Photographer
      Augie Salbosa Photography
      Honolulu, Hawaii

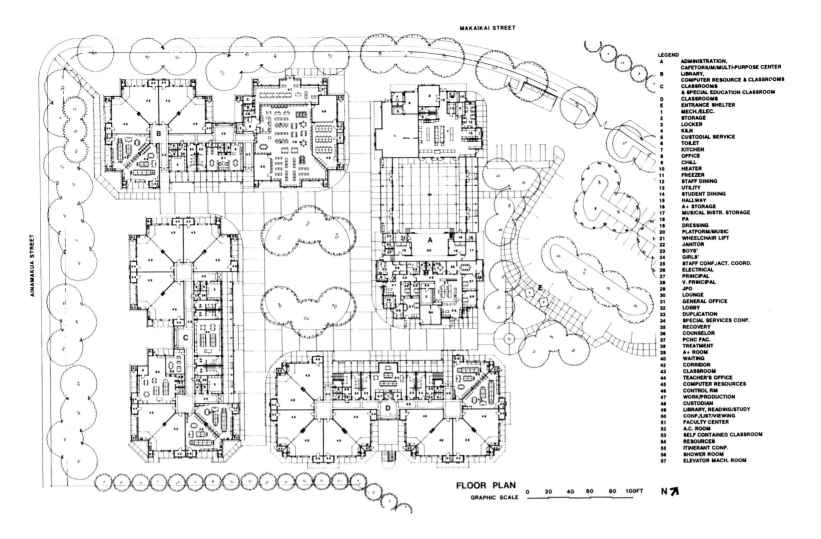

MAKAIKAI STREET

AINAMAKUA STREET

LEGEND

A ADMINISTRATION, CAFETORIUM/MULTI-PURPOSE CENTER
B LIBRARY, COMPUTER RESOURCE & CLASSROOMS
C CLASSROOMS & SPECIAL EDUCATION CLASSROOM
D CLASSROOMS
E ENTRANCE SHELTER
1 MECH./ELEC.
2 STORAGE
3 LOCKER
4 KILN
5 CUSTODIAL SERVICE
6 TOILET
7 KITCHEN
8 OFFICE
9 CHILL
10 HEATER
11 FREEZER
12 STAFF DINING
13 UTILITY
14 STUDENT DINING
15 HALLWAY
16 A+ STORAGE
17 MUSICAL INSTR. STORAGE
18 PA
19 DRESSING
20 PLATFORM/MUSIC
21 WHEELCHAIR LIFT
22 JANITOR
23 BOYS'
24 GIRLS'
25 STAFF CONF./ACT. COORD.
26 ELECTRICAL
27 PRINCIPAL
28 V. PRINCIPAL
29 JPO
30 LOUNGE
31 GENERAL OFFICE
32 LOBBY
33 DUPLICATION
34 SPECIAL SERVICES CONF.
35 RECOVERY
36 COUNSELOR
37 PCNC FAC.
38 TREATMENT
39 A+ ROOM
40 WAITING
42 CORRIDOR
43 CLASSROOM
44 TEACHER'S OFFICE
45 COMPUTER RESOURCES
46 CONTROL RM
47 WORK/PRODUCTION
48 CUSTODIAN
49 LIBRARY, READING/STUDY
50 CONF./LIST/VIEWING
51 FACULTY CENTER
52 A.C. ROOM
53 SELF CONTAINED CLASSROOM
54 RESOURCES
55 ITINERANT CONF.
56 SHOWER ROOM
57 ELEVATOR MACH. ROOM

FLOOR PLAN

GRAPHIC SCALE   0   20   40   60   80   100FT

N ↗

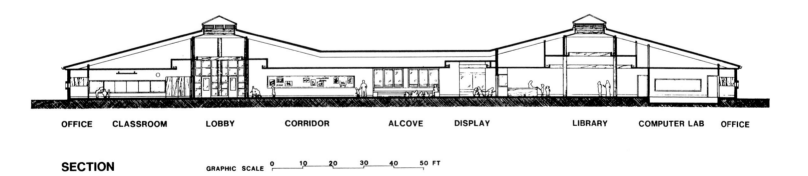

OFFICE   CLASSROOM   LOBBY   CORRIDOR   ALCOVE   DISPLAY   LIBRARY   COMPUTER LAB   OFFICE

SECTION   GRAPHIC SCALE   0   10   20   30   40   50 FT

Morton Elementary School

Hammond, Indiana

A few of the challenges for the project were to convey a warm openness, to provide flexibility, and to accommodate varying learning group sizes and learning strategies. In response, the building is composed of a series of nested organizational units: the school, the pod, the grade level cluster, and the classroom and small group spaces. There are three similar pods in the building. The scale of the building is minimized by using sloped shingled roofs representative of the sur-rounding residential community. A commitment was made to integrate the terra cotta and other sculpture from the original school into the design of the new building in order to continue the sense of tradition, artwork, and community heritage associated with the old building. Two large terra cotta statues have been reinstalled in the lobby to provide a focal point, a "sacred space," and to recall the heritage of the building.

Owner
School City of Hammond

Data

Type of Facility
Elementary school

Type of Construction
New

Area of Building
84,703 GSF

Cost of Construction
$8,288,306

Cost of Educational Equipment
$541,408

Status of Project
Completed August 1992

Credits

Architect
Fanning/Howey Associates, Inc.
114 York Street
Michigan City, Indiana 46360

Structural and Electrical Engineer
Fanning/Howey Associates, Inc.
Indianapolis, Indiana

Mechanical Engineer
Fanning/Howey Associates, Inc.
Michigan City, Indiana

Contractor
Gough, Inc.
Crown Point, Indiana

Photographer
Emery Photography
Columbus, Ohio

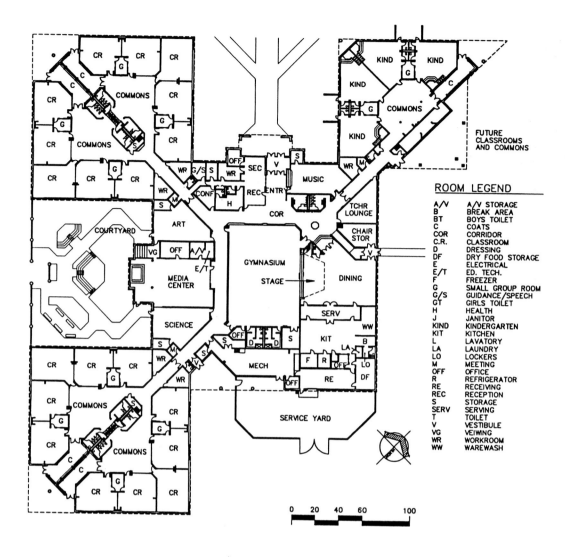

ROOM LEGEND

A/V	A/V STORAGE
B	BREAK AREA
BT	BOYS TOILET
C	COATS
COR	CORRIDOR
C.R.	CLASSROOM
D	DRESSING
DF	DRY FOOD STORAGE
E	ELECTRICAL
E/T	ED. TECH.
F	FREEZER
G	SMALL GROUP ROOM
G/S	GUIDANCE/SPEECH
GT	GIRLS TOILET
H	HEALTH
J	JANITOR
KIND	KINDERGARTEN
KIT	KITCHEN
L	LAVATORY
LA	LAUNDRY
LO	LOCKERS
M	MEETING
OFF	OFFICE
R	REFRIGERATOR
RE	RECEIVING
REC	RECEPTION
S	STORAGE
SERV	SERVING
T	TOILET
V	VESTIBULE
VG	VEIWING
WR	WORKROOM
WW	WAREWASH

0 20 40 60 100

47

Vinton Elementary School

Lafayette, Indiana

This replacement elementary school was designed to accommodate an interdisciplinary team-teaching philosophy. A pod configuration accommodates four classrooms per grade with moveable walls, a teacher planning area, and a commons area, creating a flexible and cooperative learning environment. Shared instructional facilities, including the media center and computer classroom, are grouped for central access by all grade-level pods.

The building and site are organized into two areas: activity and instructional. The activity area is at the southern end of the building, adjacent to the outdoor play areas and the main entrance. Buses and cars have separate drop-off areas. The gymnasium, platform, and cafeteria are grouped to allow for flexible scheduling of programs and to facilitate after-school community activities. Art and music classes are adjacent to the activity area and central to the pods. The centrally located administration area is located to give staff the ability to supervise the main entrance.

Owner
Lafayette School Corporation

Data
Type of Facility
Elementary school

Type of Construction
New

Area of Building
82,570 GSF

Cost of Construction
$7,462,400

Cost of Educational Equipment
N/A

Status of Project
Completed March 1994

Credits
Architect
The Odle McGuire & Shook
Corporation
8275 Allison Pointe Trail
Indianapolis, Indiana 46250

*Structural/Mechanical/Electrical
Engineer*
The Odle McGuire & Shook
Corporation
Indianapolis, Indiana

Construction Manager
Kettelhut Construction Inc.
Lafayette, Indiana

Photographer
Dan Francis, Mardan Photography
Indianapolis, Indiana

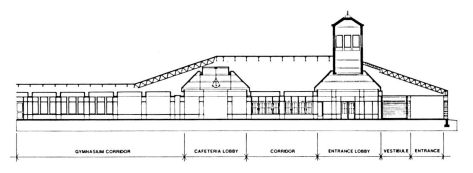

GYMNASIUM CORRIDOR | CAFETERIA LOBBY | CORRIDOR | ENTRANCE LOBBY | VESTIBULE | ENTRANCE

BUILDING SECTION 'A'

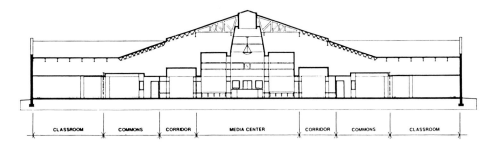

CLASSROOM | COMMONS | CORRIDOR | MEDIA CENTER | CORRIDOR | COMMONS | CLASSROOM

BUILDING SECTION 'B'

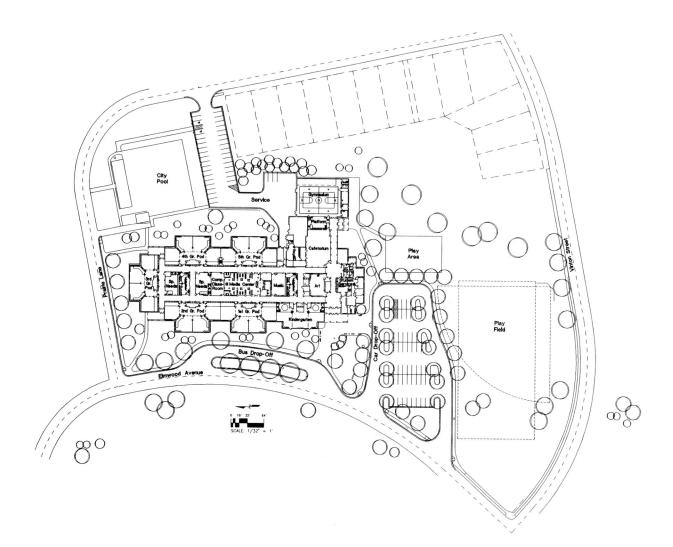

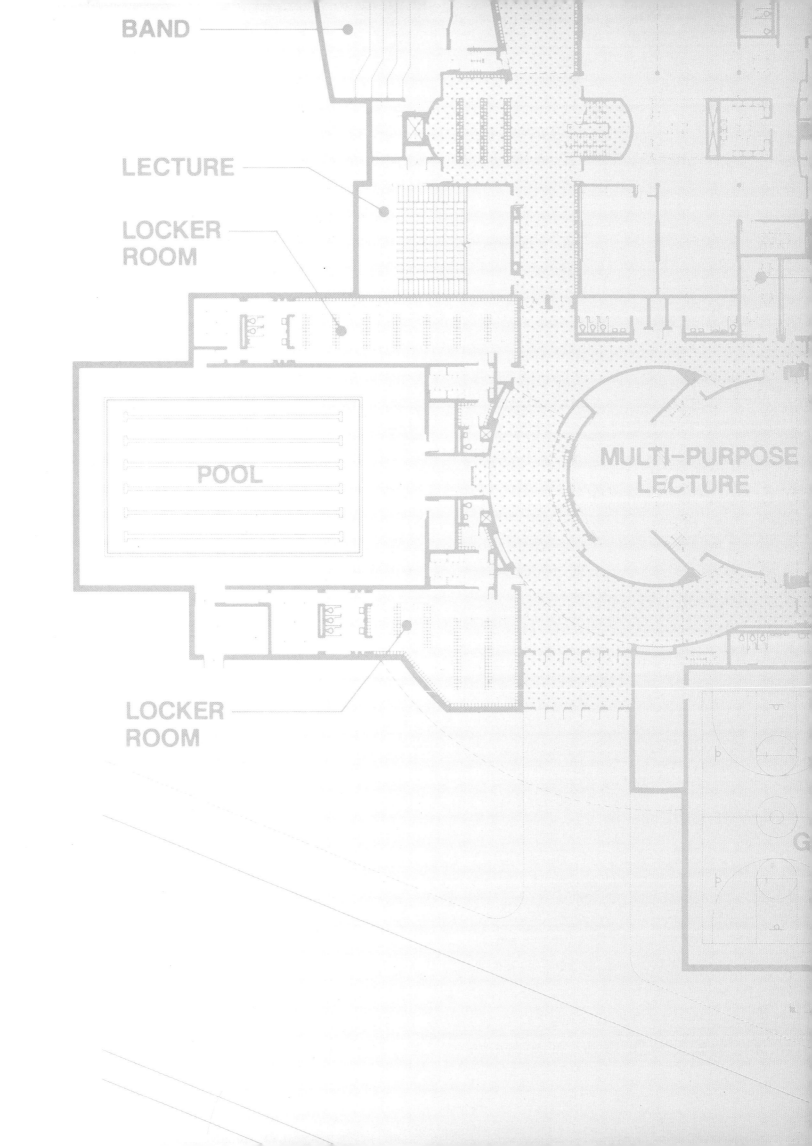

BAND

LECTURE

LOCKER
ROOM

POOL

MULTI-PURPOSE
LECTURE

LOCKER
ROOM

Intermediate Schools

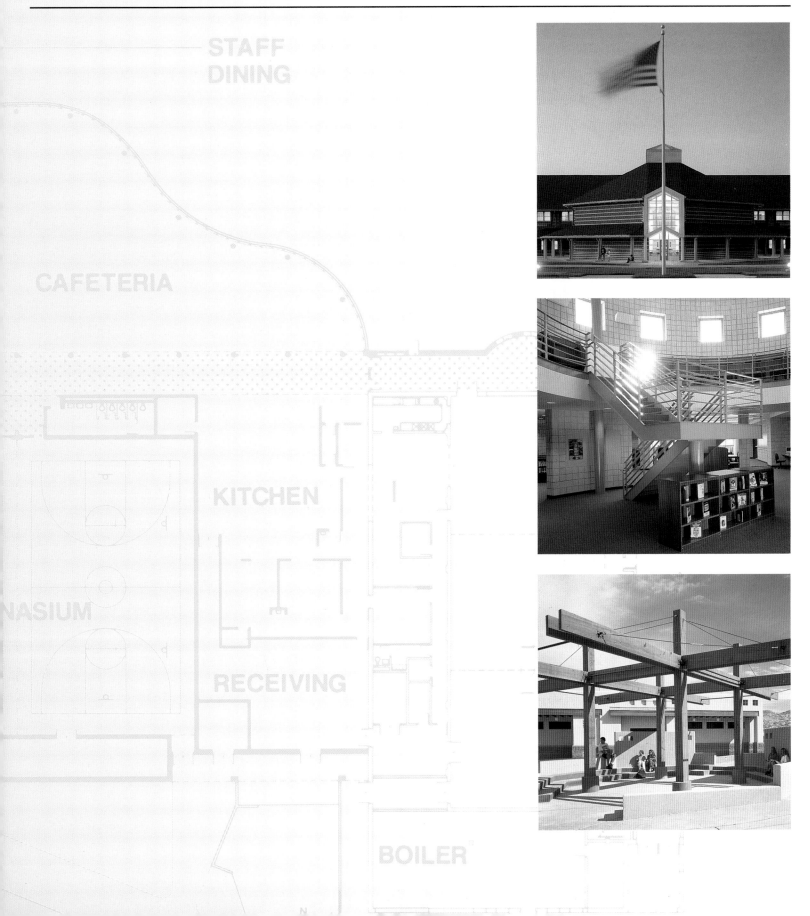

Black Hawk Middle School

Eagan, Minnesota

54

Citation

This flexible facility creates "schools within the school" with its house concept, which places students in specific areas to learn all their core subjects from a staff of four to five instructors; these instructors monitor their progress through grades 6, 7, and 8.

Within each house, a variety of classrooms and support spaces encourages interdisciplinary team teaching and flexible scheduling of lessons. The activity spaces, including the gymnasium and swimming pool, are available for use by the community, extending the benefits of the school's flexibility beyond its student population. A staff commons area responds well to the needs of the faculty.

Owner
   Independent School District #196

Data
   Type of Facility
   Middle school

   Type of Construction
   New

   Area of Building
   193,000 GSF

   Cost of Construction
   $13,815,000

   Cost of Educational Equipment
   $1,490,000

   Status of Project
   Completed July 1994

Credits
   Architect
   Wold Architects and Engineers
   6 West Fifth Street
   St. Paul, Minnesota 55102

   Structural Engineer
   Bakke Kopp Ballou & McFarlin, Inc.
   Minneapolis, Minnesota

   Mechanical/Electrical Engineer
   Wold Architects and Engineers
   St. Paul, Minnesota

   Food Service Systems Consultant
   Robert Rippe and Associates, Inc.
   Minneapolis, Minnesota

   Contractor
   Adolfson & Peterson, Inc.
   Minneapolis, Minnesota

   Photographer
   Koyama Photographic
   Minneapolis, Minnesota

ARCHITECT'S STATEMENT

This 193,000-square-foot facility was designed to deliver educational services to 1,200 students in grades six through eight. The school's eight identical houses are organized into three 3-story towers along one side of the school's north wing. A skylit atrium, referred to as "the street," divides the houses from the administrative offices, band room, choir room, and media center located on the opposite side of the wing. The student entry at the south end of "the street" links the houses and support spaces with the school's physical education, auditorium, and cafeteria facilities.

With the house concept, students waste less time moving between classes, benefit from constant exposure to a core group of teachers, and enjoy a social environment better suited to the emotional needs of early adolescence. The physical environment of Black Hawk Middle School has been created to improve delivery of educational services and student performance; the school gives physical form to an educational philosophy.

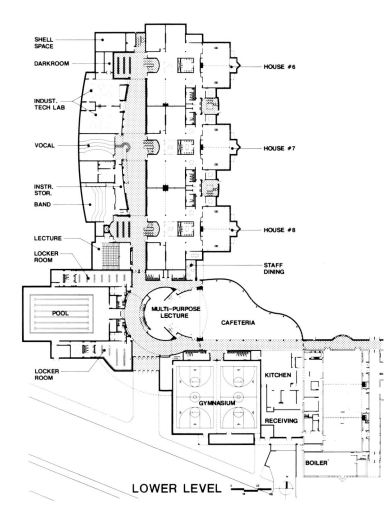

SHELL
SPACE

DARKROOM

HOUSE #6

INDUST.
TECH LAB

VOCAL

HOUSE #7

INSTR.
STOR.

BAND

HOUSE #8

LECTURE

LOCKER
ROOM

STAFF
DINING

MULTI-PURPOSE
LECTURE

POOL

CAFETERIA

LOCKER
ROOM

KITCHEN

GYMNASIUM

RECEIVING

BOILER

LOWER LEVEL

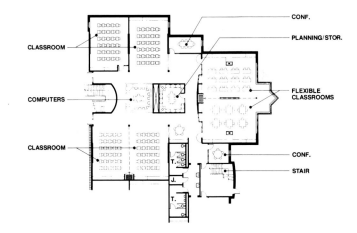

CONF.

PLANNING/STOR.

CLASSROOM

FLEXIBLE
CLASSROOMS

COMPUTERS

CLASSROOM

CONF.

STAIR

T.

J.

T.

TYPICAL HOUSE

Barrington Middle School–"Prairie Campus"

Barrington, Illinois

ARCHITECT'S STATEMENT

This new middle school accommodates flexible organizational and teaching strategies. Team teaching environments including staff and small group areas are supported by a mid-level learning center offering equal access to all students.

The building design incorporates two entries with distinct "student" and "visitor" identities, sharing a central administrative core. The infrastructure accommodates 1,000 students for planned growth. Existing wetlands and prairie plantings were enhanced and turned into an attractive, low-maintenance outdoor classroom. A voice, video, and data system incorporated throughout the school uses technology to fully integrate the educational program between classrooms and beyond the building's walls.

Owner
Community Unit School District #220

Data

Type of Facility
Middle school

Type of Construction
New

Area of Building
125,000 GSF

Cost of Construction
$8,517,300

Status of Project
Completed August 1992

Credits

Architect
Ruck/Pate Architecture
257 East Main Street
Barrington, Illinois 60010

Structural Engineer
Sheffee Lulkin & Associates, Inc.
Skokie, Illinois

Mechanical/Electrical Engineer
Consolidated Consulting Engineers
Wheeling, Illinois

Wetlands Consultant
Applied Ecological Services
Brodhead, Wisconsin

Landscape Architecture
David R. McCallum Associates, Inc.
Libertyville, Illinois

Contractor
Camosy, Incorporated
Waukegan, Illinois

Photographer
Mark A. Samuels
Deerfield, Illinois

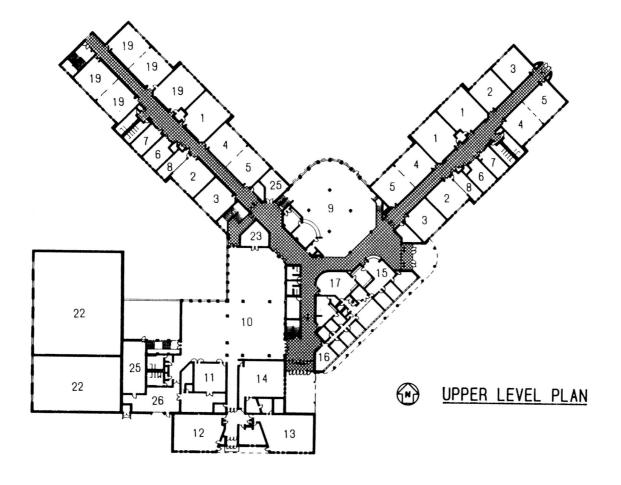

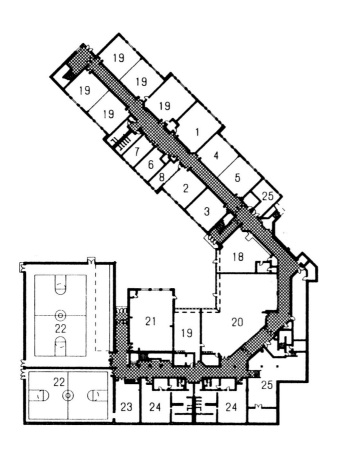

1. Science Classroom
2. Mathematics Classroom
3. Foreign Language Classroom
4. English Classroom
5. Social Studies Classroom
6. Special Education Classroom
7. Teachers Planning Room
8. Computer Lab
9. Learning Center
10. Commons
11. Kitchen
12. Orchestra Room
13. Band Room
14. Choral Music
15. Main Office
16. Guidance Office
17. Staff Lounge
18. Art
19. Classroom
20. Technology Center
21. Home Economics
22. Gymnasium
23. Storage
24. Locker Room
25. Mechanical
26. Receiving

UPPER LEVEL PLAN

LOWER LEVEL PLAN

Chippens Hill Middle School

Bristol, Connecticut

ARCHITECT'S STATEMENT

This new middle school is a three-story, 166,215 square-foot facility housing 900 students in grades six, seven and eight. The programmatic intent was to create independent, team-teaching clusters of academic classrooms while allowing future flexibility for non-team educational models. At the same time, the program needed to be contained within an efficient and compact building that integrates core facilities and unifies arts with academics.

The building is divided into three zones running its length. Teams consist of nine 5-room clusters extending along the east zone, overlooking a wood area maximizing natural lights and views. The two-story middle zone includes the large auditorium, gymnasium, cafeteria, and library spaces.

O w n e r
City of Bristol

D a t a
Type of Facility
Middle school

Type of Construction
New

Area of Building
166,215 GSF

Cost of Construction
$13,076,000

Cost of Educational Equipment
$354,800

Status of Project
Completed 1993

C r e d i t s
Architect
Stecker LaBau Arneill McManus
80 Glastonbury Boulevard
Glastonbury, Connecticut
06033-4400

*Structural/Mechanical/Electrical
Engineer*
BVH
Bloomfield, Connecticut

(credits continue)

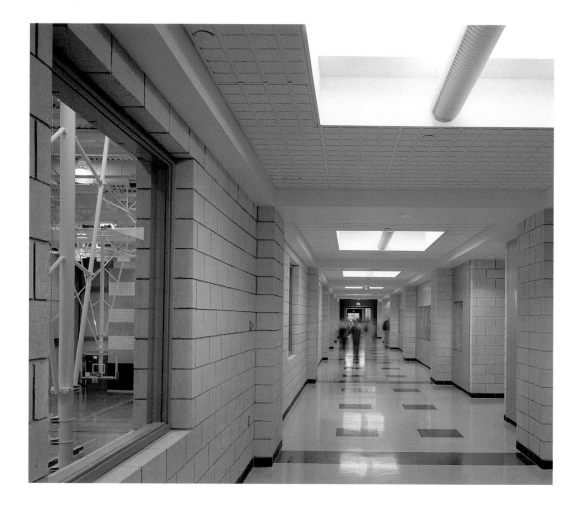

Credits (continued)

Civil Engineer
Purcell Engineers
Glastonbury, Connecticut

Land Surveying
Aeschliman Land Surveying
Glastonbury, Connecticut

Soils/Lab Engineering
Haley & Aldrich
Glastonbury, Connecticut

Contractor
Atlas-SCI (a joint venture)
Bristol, Connecticut

Photographer
Wheeler Photographics
Weston, Massachusetts

Site Plan Photographer
Woodruff/Brown
West Hartford, Connecticut

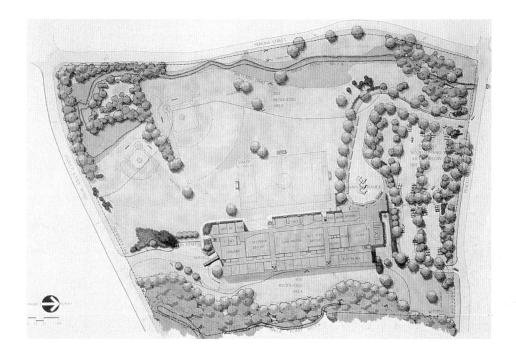

Chisholm Trail Intermediate School

Keller, Texas

ARCHITECT'S STATEMENT

The metal clad "wing" and translucent paneled clerestory rising above the facility's main spine defines the visual character of the building, while providing a light-filled organizational link between academic areas. The program requirements, developed to accommodate 1,200 students and function as a fifth and sixth grade school, are arranged in classroom clusters, equally divided between two floors, allowing separation between grades. Shared community functions (cafetorium, gymnasiums, music) are located at the opposite end of the facility providing noise separation. Other academic and administrative facilities are located along the spine for easy access to all levels.

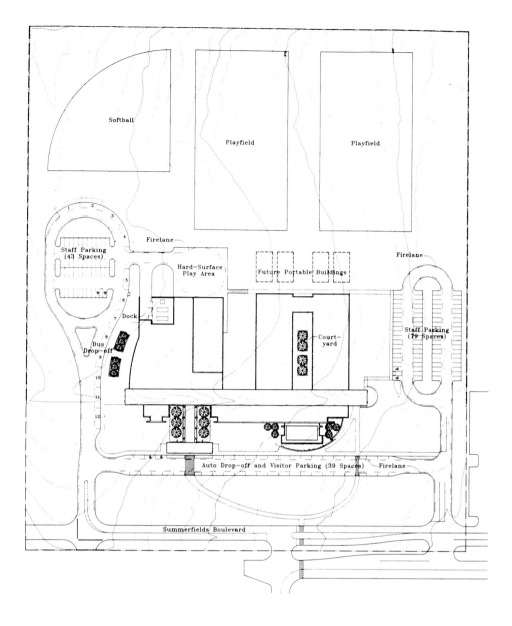

SITE PLAN

Softball

Playfield

Playfield

Staff Parking
(43 Spaces)

Firelane

Hard-Surface
Play Area

Future Portable Buildings

Firelane

Dock

Court-
yard

Staff Parking
(79 Spaces)

Bus
Drop-off

Auto Drop-off and Visitor Parking (39 Spaces)

Firelane

Summerfields Boulevard

Owner
  Keller Independent School District

Data
  Type of Facility
  Intermediate school

  Type of Construction
  New

  Area of Building
  123,164 GSF

  Cost of Construction
  $6,930,079

  Cost of Furniture and Equipment
  $400,000

  Status of Project
  Completed August 1994

Credits
  Architect
  Hahnfeld Associates
  Architects/Planners, Inc.
  675 North Henderson, Suite 100
  Fort Worth, Texas 76107

  Structural Engineer
  Metro Structural
  Hurst, Texas

  Mechanical/Electrical Engineer
  Reed, Wells, Benson & Co.
  Dallas, Texas

(credits continue)

Credits (continued)

Landscape Architect
Oliver Windham
Arlington, Texas

Food Services Consultant
H.G. Rice and Company, Inc.
Irving, Texas

Contractor
Buford Thompson Company
Arlington, Texas

Photographer
Michael Lyon
Dallas, Texas

Intermediate Schools

Roberto Clemente Middle School

Philadelphia, Pennsylvania

ARCHITECT'S STATEMENT

Conceptually the building was envisioned as an academic village embracing a secured courtyard. The village concept allowed us to reduce the scale of this otherwise large building by breaking it into five connected structures holding the various educational components: an academic wing, art/specialty classrooms, auditorium, gymnasium, and kitchen/cafeteria. The courtyard serves as an identifiable gathering place encouraging a sense of community open to a variety of uses. The position and massing of the various elements signify their relationship to school and community while lively colors, patterns and forms lend the building character and create a more intimate and appropriate scale for both school and neighborhood residents.

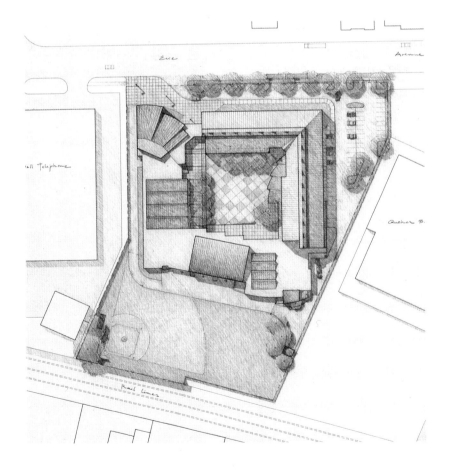

O w n e r
  Philadelphia School District

D a t a

  Type of Facility
    Middle school

  Type of Construction
    New

  Area of Building
    165,711 GSF

  Cost of Construction
    $16,200,000

  Cost of Educational Equipment
    $600,000

  Status of Project
    Completed January 1995

C r e d i t s

  Architect
    Agoos/Lovera Architects
    731 South Broad Street
    Philadelphia, Pennsylvania 19147

  Associate Architect
    Polatnick & Zacharjasz Architects
    7870 Spring Avenue
    Elkins Park, Pennsylvania 19027

  Structural Engineer
    Christakis, VanOcker, Morrison
    Upper Darby, Pennsylvania

  Mechanical/Electrical Engineer
    Vinokur-Pace Engineering Services
    Jenkintown, Pennsylvania

  Civil Engineering/Landscape
    Cairone and Kaupp, Inc.
    Philadelphia, Pennsylvania

  Food Service Consultant
    John L. Manning, F.C.S.I.
    Dresher, Pennsylvania

  Cost Consultant
    Arena and Company
    Wallingford, Pennsylvania

  Construction Manager
    Daniel J. Keating Company, Inc.
    Ardmore, Pennsylvania

  Photographer
    Peter Olson
    Philadelphia, Pennsylvania

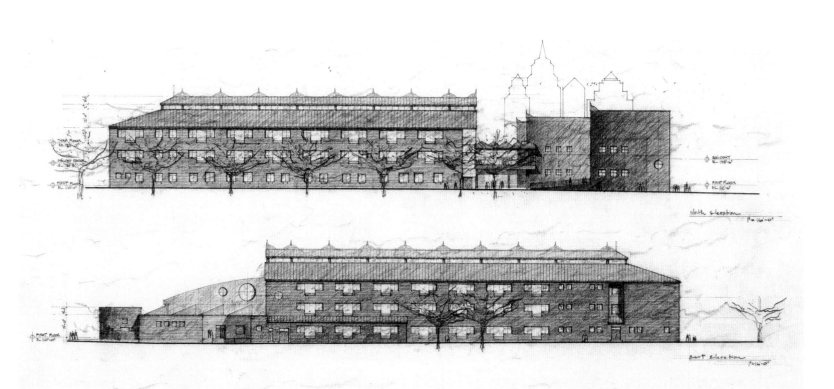

Greenfield Junior High

Gilbert, Arizona

ARCHITECT'S STATEMENT

The organizing concept for the campus is the central courtyard, which was conceived as a large space designed to accommodate the boundless energy of junior-high-school age children. Students are able to leave the confines of the buildings and enter the courtyard to run, talk, and enjoy each other's company before reentering the more controlled and subdued environment of the academic structures. The triangular courtyard is expansive enough that students can experience the mild Arizona winters without feeling confined, yet the shape allows administration to monitor the space with a minimum of staff.

Owner
Gilbert Unified School District #41

Data

Type of Facility
Junior high school

Type of Construction
New

Area of Building
158,860 GSF

Cost of Construction
$9,404,430

Status of Project
Completed August 1994

Credits

Architect
Hofmann-Dietz Architects, Ltd.
1400 East Southern Avenue,
Suite 460
Tempe, Arizona 85282

Structural Engineer
Robin E. Parke Associates
Phoenix, Arizona

Mechanical Engineer
Pearson Engineering Associates Inc.
Phoenix, Arizona

Electrical Engineer
Hofmann-Dietz Architects, Ltd.
Tempe, Arizona

Civil Engineer
Keith W. Hubbard
Gilbert, Arizona

Landscape Architect
G.K. Flanagan Associates
Phoenix, Arizona

Food Service Consultant
Reed/Hedberg Restaurant Design &
Equipment
Phoenix, Arizona

Contractor
D.L. Withers Construction, Inc.
Tempe, Arizona

Photographers
Richard Abrams
Phoenix, Arizona

Jon Anderson, A.I.A.
Tempe, Arizona

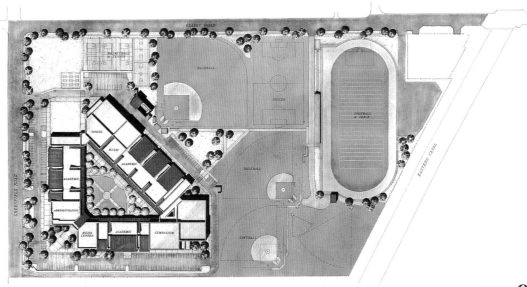

SITE PLAN

LEGEND

A. ADMINISTRATION CENTER
B. CLASSROOM
C. MEDIA CENTER
D. GYMNASIUM
E. STUDENT DINING
F. BAND ROOM
G. CHORUS ROOM
H. STRINGS
I. SCIENCE LAB
J. FACULTY OFFICE
K. SPECIAL EDUCATION
L. WRESTLING / DANCE
M. WEIGHT ROOM
N. PE LOCKER ROOM
O. FOOD LAB
P. SEWING LAB
Q. TECHNOLOGY
R. ART LAB
S. STORAGE
T. KITCHEN
U. FACULTY DINING
V. EXTERIOR COURTYARD

FLOOR PLAN

0 5' 15'   30'   50'

Lake Powell School

Page, Arizona

ARCHITECT'S STATEMENT

All students at the Lake Powell School have an unobstructed view of the lake as they approach the campus' central spine that runs from the parking lot and extends to the lake. This central spine is symbolic of a boat dock and acts as a collector to organize pedestrian circulation to each of the buildings which are like boats parked at the dock. At the center of the dock is a true scale Anasazi Indian kiva that is used as an outdoor classroom and accommodates community activities.

National Parks require that no construction occur on undisturbed natural land. So the school had to be constructed on an abandoned, drained sewer lagoon. All structures must "fit" the site and blend into the environment. The exterior color bands of stucco and masonry echo the surrounding rock stratifications and horizontal formations.

The design was influenced by additional community requirements such as wedding receptions, campfire lectures, community athletics, historical artifacts displays, and adult distance learning programs.

Owner
National Park Service

Data

Type of Facility
K-12 public school

Type of Construction
New

Area of Building
20,802 GSF

Cost of Construction
$1,070,000

Cost of Educational Equipment
$75,000

Status of Project
Completed August 1995

Credits

Architect
Valentiner Crane Brunjes Onyon
Architects
524 South 600 East
Salt Lake City, Utah 84102

Structural Engineer
McNeil Engineering
Salt Lake City, Utah

Mechanical Engineer
Bennion Engineering
Salt Lake City, Utah

Electrical Engineer
BNA Consulting Engineers
Salt Lake City, Utah

Landscape Architects
Webster & Associates
Salt Lake City, Utah

Contractor
Hogan & Tingey
Salt Lake City, Utah

Photographer
Scot Zimmerman
Park City, Utah

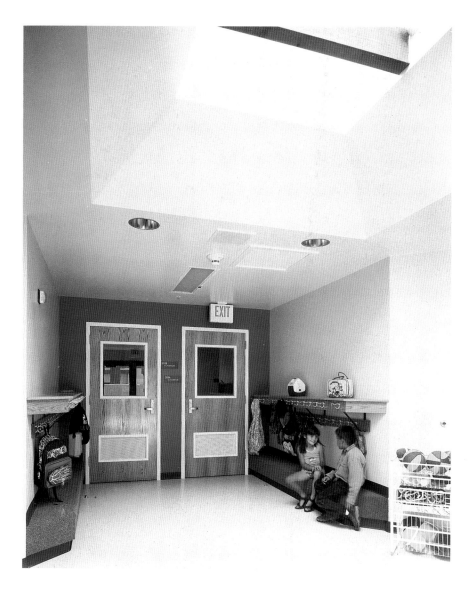

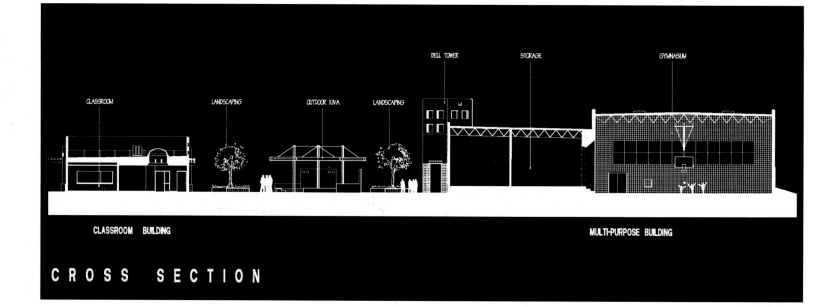

CLASSROOM   LANDSCAPING   OUTDOOR KIVA   LANDSCAPING   BELL TOWER   STORAGE   GYMNASIUM

CLASSROOM BUILDING   MULTI-PURPOSE BUILDING

CROSS SECTION

Walled Lake Middle School

Walled Lake, Michigan

This new middle school is designed around the media center as the symbolic focus of learning. This focus, with its distinctive roof form and skylight, defines the main entry to the school, and its placement at the heart of the two-level academic cluster enables it to truly be the "town center" for the students. Reinforcing this organization are two major student commons: one directly adjacent to the media center, and all specialized areas around the other. These commons provide a social space for students, and their placement facilitates "friendly" supervision by staff. A unique feature adjacent to the classrooms is the "mini-tech" lab which is used to foster individualized learning opportunities with the use of the computer. Each class area is linked directly to the media center via voice, video, and data connections.

Owner
    Walled Lake Consolidated School District

Data
Type of Facility
    Middle school

Type of Construction
    New

Area of Building
    144,500 GSF

Cost of Construction
    $12,731,480

Cost of Educational Equipment
    $229,134

Status of Project
    Completed September 1992

(credits continue)

Credits

Architect

> TMP Associates, Inc.
> 1191 West Square Lake Road
> Bloomfield Hills, Michigan 48302

Structural/Mechanical/Electrical Engineer

> TMP Associates, Inc.
> Bloomfield Hills, Michigan

Landscape Architect

> Paul T. Nakolan & Design
> Associates
> Union Lake, Michigan

Cost Estimator

> Jeffsan, Inc.
> West Bloomfield, Michigan

Educational Planner

> Ben E. Graves, Hon. AIA
> Austin, Texas

Contractor

> George W. Auch Co.
> Pontiac, Michigan

Photographer

> Gary Quesada, Balthazar Korab, Ltd.
> Troy, Michigan

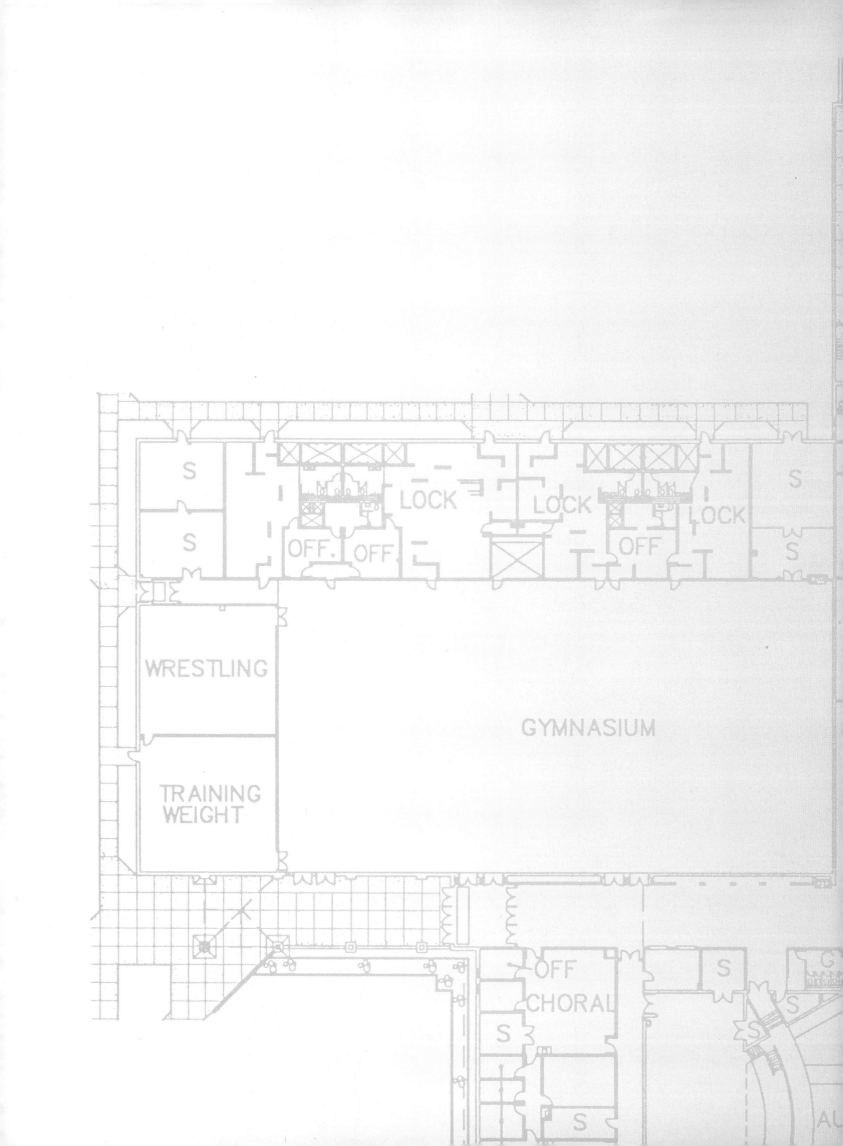

High Schools

P. W. Johansen High School

Modesto, California

Citation

This new high school boasts excellent athletic facilities, an Olympic-sized pool, an amphitheater, a well-developed external courtyard, efficient circulation, and a campus design that responds to its agricultural surroundings. A new bell tower housing the original school's bell is symbolic of the school's role as a community center, used extensively for fine arts presentations and similar gatherings.

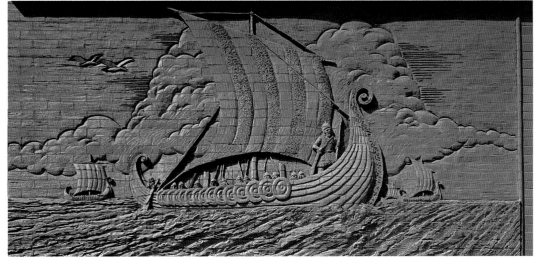

Owner
Modesto City Schools

Data

Type of Facility
High school

Type of Construction
New

Area of Building
225,000 GSF

Cost of Construction
$40,000,000

Status of Project
Completed September 1992

Credits

Architect
Wolff/Lang/Christopher
Architects, Inc.
10470 Foothill Boulevard
Rancho Cucamonga,
California 91730

Structural Engineer
Johnson & Nielsen Associates
Riverside, California

Mechanical Engineer
F.T. Andrews, Inc.
Anaheim, California

Electrical Engineer
M/P Engineers, Inc.
Fullerton, California

Civil Engineer
Lew-Garcia-Davis
Ceres, California

Landscape Architect
Land Images
Marina del Rey, California

Kitchen Consultant
Commercial Kitchen Design
La Canada-Flintridge, California

Contractor
Roebbelen Construction, Inc.
El Dorado Hills, California

Photographer
Architectural Specialties Studio
(No longer in business)

ARCHITECT'S STATEMENT

On a relatively isolated 100-acre site, the architect designed a complex that would "reinforce the community's agricultural heritage" by retaining a one-acre preserve at the school's entrance and a 20-foot wide buffer of trees around the site.

A county library, theater, football stadium, Olympic-size swimming pool, tennis courts, and playing fields were integrated into the 225,000-square-foot, $40 million school. To convey community stature and educational energy, the architects devised two-story steel-framed volumes clad in brick and arranged around an outdoor courtyard linked by walkways.

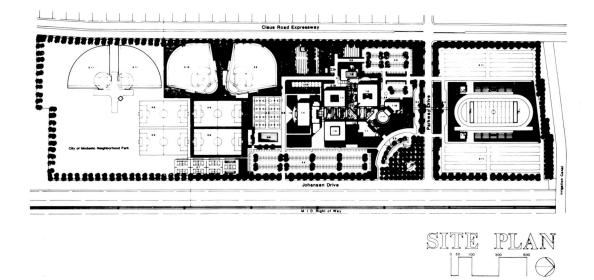

SITE PLAN

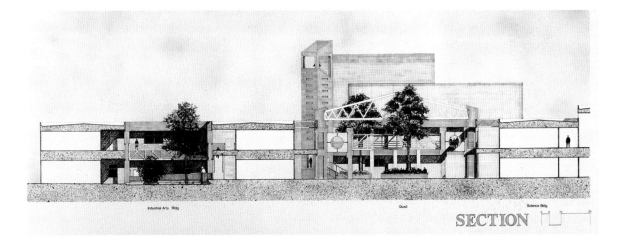

SECTION

Eastlake High School

Chula Vista, California

ARCHITECT'S STATEMENT

The site is defined by steep topography with a Pacific Ocean view. The high school houses joint school/community fine arts, park, and athletic facilities. A technology curriculum is emphasized. The pro- ject features an urban village planning design, with a campus organized along a cross axis. At the axial inter- section of the malls, there is green turf defined by building edges, arcade rhythms, and tree bosques.

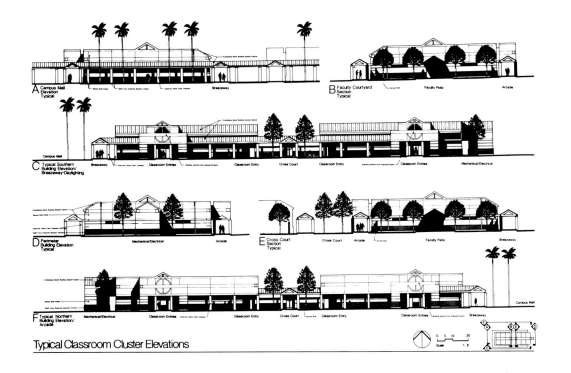

A Campus Mall Elevation Typical   Breezeway

B Faculty Courtyard Section Typical   Faculty Patio   Arcade

C Typical Southern Building Elevation/ Breezeway-Daylighting   Breezeway   Classroom Entries   Classroom Entry   Cross Court   Classroom Entry   Classroom Entries   Mechanical/Electrical

D Perimeter Building Elevation Typical   Mechanical/Electrical   Arcade

E Cross Court Section Typical   Cross Court   Arcade   Faculty Patio   Breezeway

F Typical Northern Building Elevation/ Arcade   Mechanical/Electrical   Classroom Entries   Classroom Entry   Cross Court   Classroom Entry   Classroom Entries   Breezeway   Campus Mall

Typical Classroom Cluster Elevations

Owner
Sweetwater Union High School District

Data

Type of Facility
High school

Type of Construction
New

Area of Building
252,657 GSF

Cost of Construction
$35,618,000

Cost of Educational Equipment
$ 2,434,370

Status of Project
Completed November 1994

Credits

Architect
Ruhnau Ruhnau Associates
5751 Palmer Way, Suite C
Carlsbad, California 92008

3775 Tenth Street
Riverside, California 99501

Structural Engineer
Brandow & Johnston Associates
Los Angeles, California

Mechanical Engineer
Nack Engineering
San Clemente, California

Electrical Engineer
Frederick Brown Associates
Newport Beach, California

Landscape Architect
WYA Landscape Architects
San Diego, California

Performing Arts Consultant
John Von Szeliski, AIA
Newport Beach, California

Contractor
Centex-Golden Construction Company
San Diego, California

Photographer
Wayne Thorn
Los Angeles, California

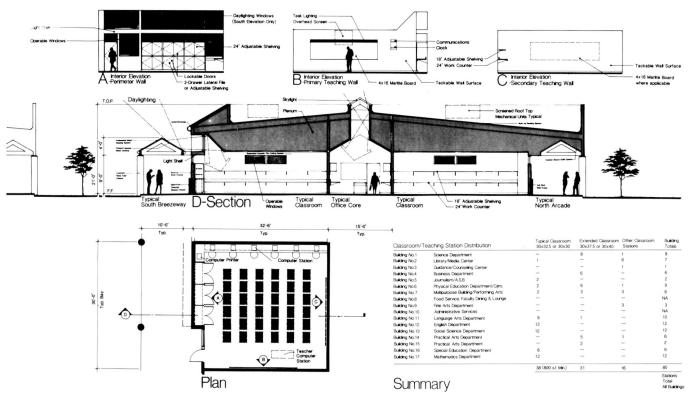

Classroom/Teaching Station Distribution		Typical Classroom 30x32.5 or 30x30	Extended Classroom 30x37.5 or 30x40	Other Classroom Stations	Building Totals
Building No.1	Science Department	—	8	1	9
Building No.2	Library/Media Center	1	—	6	7
Building No.3	Guidance/Counseling Center	—	—	1	1
Building No.4	Business Department	—	6	—	6
Building No.5	Journalism/A.S.B.	2	—	—	2
Building No.6	Physical Education Department/Gym	2	6	1	9
Building No.7	Multipurpose Building/Performing Arts	2	3	3	8
Building No.8	Food Service, Faculty Dining & Lounge	—	—	—	NA
Building No.9	Fine Arts Department	—	—	3	3
Building No.10	Administrative Services	—	—	—	NA
Building No.11	Language Arts Department	9	1	—	10
Building No.12	English Department	12	—	—	12
Building No.13	Social Science Department	12	—	—	12
Building No.14	Practical Arts Department	—	5	1	6
Building No.15	Practical Arts Department	—	2	—	2
Building No.16	Special Education Department	6	—	—	6
Building No.17	Mathematics Department	12	—	—	12
		38 (800 s.f. Min.)	31	16	85
					Stations Total All Buildings

Plan

Summary

Typical Classroom

RESTROOMS

LIBRARY

COPY MACHINES

Gaylord High School

Gaylord, Michigan

ARCHITECT'S STATEMENT

This comprehensive high school is designed to serve approximately 1,100 students in grades nine through twelve. An important consideration in the planning process was to serve a community which is very accomplished in music and drama, both among the school-age citizens and those who are older. Another goal was to integrate the vocational program and career technology programs with the other academic areas—science and math were the most closely connected, but it was very important to include language arts and social studies and the related instructional media center.

This building was the keystone of a districtwide educational technology development program that provides voice, video, and data systems in all buildings in support of a newly improved curriculum. The facility serves as a true community center for all ages of Gaylord community residents.

Owner
   Gaylord Community Schools

Data
   Type of Facility
   High school

   Type of Construction
   New

   Area of Building
   190,853 GSF

   Cost of Construction
   $14,816,828

   Cost of Educational Equipment
   $533,801

   Status of Project
   Completed September 1994

Credits
   Architect
      Fanning/Howey Associates, Inc.
      114 York Street
      Michigan City, Indiana 46360

   Structural Engineer
      Lawson Fisher Associates, Inc.
      South Bend, Indiana

   Mechanical Engineer
      Fanning/Howey Associates, Inc.
      Michigan City, Indiana

   Electrical Engineer
      R.L. Millies & Associates, Inc.
      Munster, Indiana

   Construction Manager
      E & V, Inc.
      Houghton Lake, Michigan

   Photographer
      Emery Photography
      Columbus, Ohio

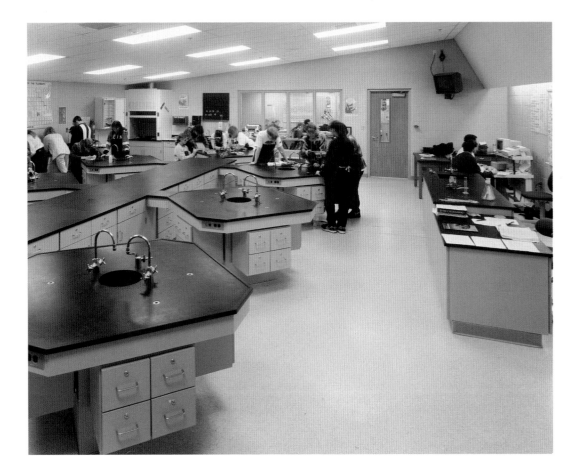

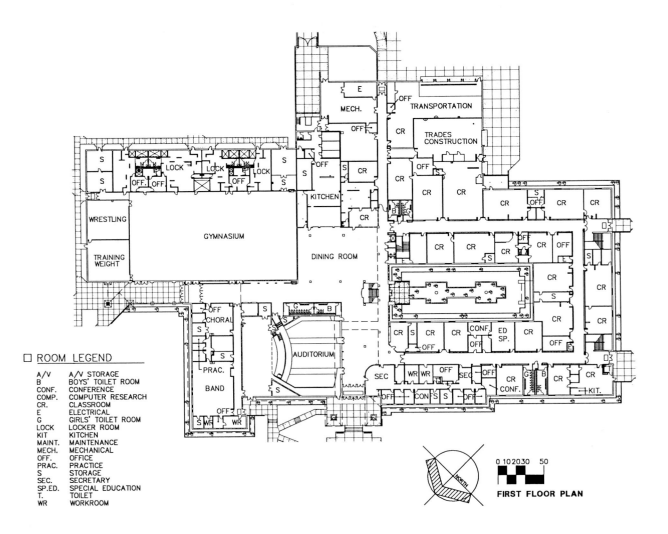

☐ ROOM LEGEND

A/V	A/V STORAGE
B	BOYS' TOILET ROOM
CONF.	CONFERENCE
COMP.	COMPUTER RESEARCH
CR.	CLASSROOM
E	ELECTRICAL
G	GIRLS' TOILET ROOM
LOCK	LOCKER ROOM
KIT	KITCHEN
MAINT.	MAINTENANCE
MECH.	MECHANICAL
OFF.	OFFICE
PRAC.	PRACTICE
S	STORAGE
SEC.	SECRETARY
SP.ED.	SPECIAL EDUCATION
T.	TOILET
WR	WORKROOM

0 10 20 30 50

FIRST FLOOR PLAN

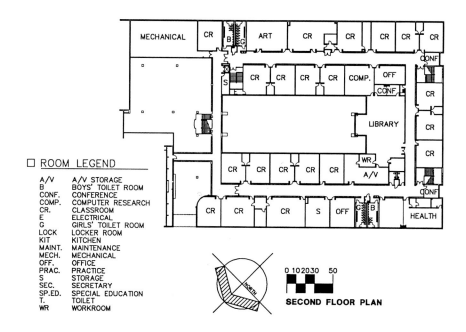

0 10 20 30   50

SECOND FLOOR PLAN

MECHANICAL   CR   B G   ART   CR   CR   CR   CR   CR

CONF

CR   CR   CR   CR   COMP.   OFF

CONF

S

LIBRARY

CR

CR

CR   CR   CR   CR   CR   WR

A/V

CONF

CR   CR   CR   S   OFF   G B

HEALTH

Gordon H. Garrett Academy of Technology

North Charleston, South Carolina

ARCHITECT'S STATEMENT

An out-of-date, mid-1950s high school was converted into the Southeast's foremost magnet high school with an imaginative 110,000 square foot addition. The new magnet high school's program required educational space for traditional curricula, as well as technological areas, including laboratories for masonry education, automotive repair, graphic design, child care, and other specialized techniques. Due to the ever-changing technological world, the building's design had to incorporate anticipated future changes in computers and machinery. Therefore, the laboratories had to not only be functional, but adaptable as well. The exterior materials were specifically chosen to reflect a high-tech appearance, foreshadowing the type of education provided within.

Owner
Charleston County School District

Data
Type of Facility
High school

Type of Construction
Combined (80 percent new,
20 percent renovation)

Area of Building
143,000 GSF (110,000 new,
33,000 renovation)

Cost of Construction
$6,400,000 ($4,700,000 new,
$1,700,000 renovation)

Cost of Educational Equipment
$700,000

Status of Project
Completed August 1994

Credits
Architect
Rosenblum & Associates
Architects, Inc.
121 Wentworth Street
Charleston, South Carolina 29401

(credits continue)

Credits (continued)

Structural Engineer

Shoolbred Engineers, Inc.
Charleston, South Carolina

Mechanical/Electrical Engineer

Owens & Associates, Inc.
Charleston, South Carolina

Civil Engineer

E.M. Seabrook, Jr., Inc.
Mount Pleasant, South Carolina

Contractor

Hill Construction Corporation
North Charleston, South Carolina

Photographer

Gordon H. Schenk, Jr.
Charlotte, North Carolina

(before aerial photo)
Larry Workman Photography
Charleston, South Carolina

(after aerial photo)
American Images
Marshfield, Wisconsin

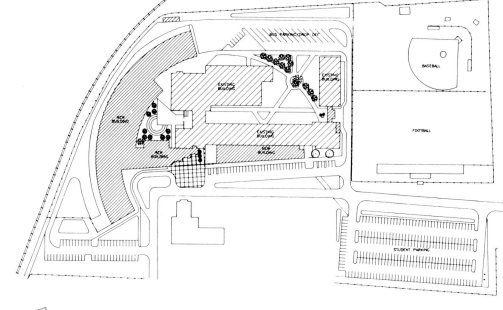

SITE PLAN

0 40 160'
20 80

SCALE: 1'=160'

High Schools

New Southwest High School

Tucson, Arizona

Vault Section / Media Center Elevation

ARCHITECT'S STATEMENT

The design of this new high school responds to several goals and objectives: flexible classroom space; direct entry to gymnasium, theater and media center; visible "front door"; community focus; and expandability.

Organized around the central common area, the "Atrio," the school shares it resources openly with the community it serves. Traditionally, in historic Southwest architecture, the Atrio was the central gathering place in front of the town church. It was used for instruction, music, dance and processions, and was the focus of community life. The characteristics of the Atrio are very appropriate to a high school environment that fosters a strong and lasting sense of community.

Building forms were derived to respond to site influences and to create flexible and expandable learning environments. Access to gymnasium and theater spaces from the Atrio will allow expansion to occur to the south as programs and enrollments enlarge. Classrooms were designed to be flexible to allow teaming, cooperative learning, and interdisciplinary teaching to occur.

Owner
  Tucson Unified School District

Data
  Type of Facility
  High school

  Type of Construction
  New

  Area of Building
  240,000 GSF

  Cost of Construction
  $19,700,000 (estimated)

  Cost of Educational Equipment
  $1,000,000 (estimated)

  Status of Project
  Date of completion not determined

Credits
  Architect
  TMP Associates, Inc.
  1191 West Square Lake Road
  Bloomfield Hills, Michigan 48302

  Associated Architects
  The IEF Group, Inc.
  705 North Seventh Avenue
  Tucson, Arizona 85705

  Structural Engineer
  Holben, Martin & White
  Tucson, Arizona

  Mechanical Engineer
  Adams & Associates, Inc.
  Tucson, Arizona

  Electrical Engineer
  Monrad Engineering, Inc.
  Tucson, Arizona

  Acoustical/Theater Arts Consultant
  Fred Masino
  Newport Beach, California

  Landscape Architect
  Cella Barr & Associates
  Tucson, Arizona

  Food Service Consultant
  E.F. Whitney, Inc.
  Birmingham, Michigan

  Contractor
  Not yet determined

  Photographer
  Gary Quesada, Balthazar Korab
  Troy, Michigan

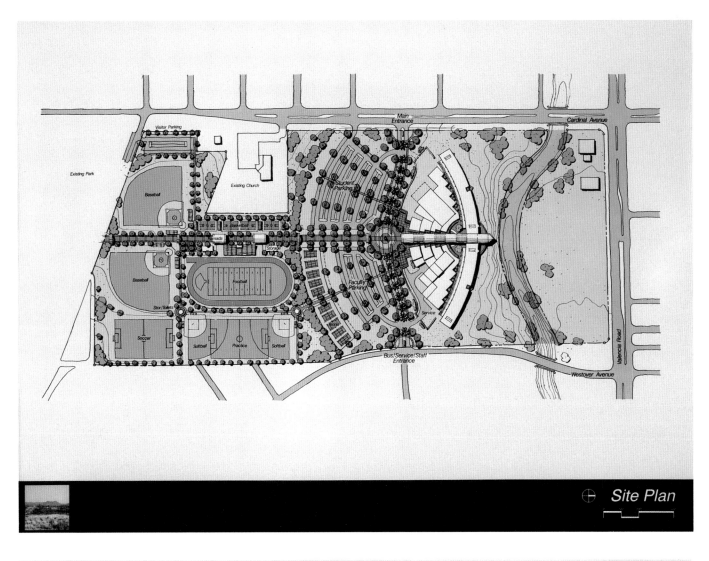

Site Plan

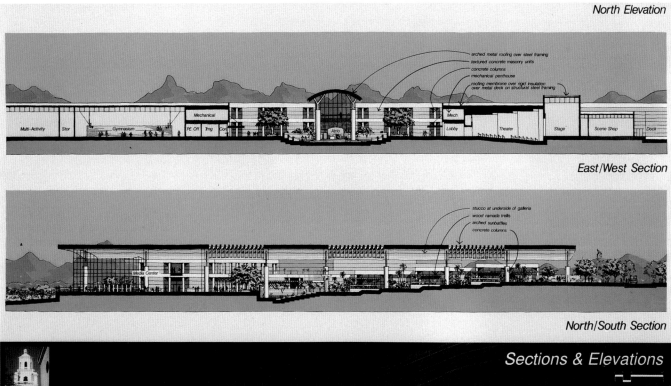

North Elevation

arched metal roofing over steel framing
textured concrete masonry units
concrete columns
mechanical penthouse
roofing membrane over rigid insulation over metal deck on structural steel framing

East/West Section

stucco at underside of galleria
wood ramada trellis
arched sunbaffles
concrete columns

North/South Section

Sections & Elevations

Rockford High School

Rockford, Michigan

ARCHITECT'S STATEMENT

In contrast to the historic proportions and design of the architecture, this new facility incorporates state-of-the-art technology and communications systems.

The building was given three primary entrances: academic, performing arts/auditorium and sports complex. All entries are linked by a central circulation concourse. This two-story concourse, which begins at the sports complex and ends at the media center, acts as a major link to the public core areas of the building. The multi-storied media center, the focal point at the end of the concourse, was designed as the computer and integrated technology hub.

Flexibility to accommodate changes in teaching methods and curriculum delivery, as well as the ability to expand the facility, were critical to the project.

Owner
Rockford Public Schools

Data
Type of Facility
High school

Type of Construction
New

Area of Building
371,012 GSF

Cost of Construction
$29,004,500

Cost of Educational Equipment
$4,121,300

Status of Project
Completed January 1993

Credits
Architect
Greiner, Inc.
3950 Sparks Drive SE
Grand Rapids, Michigan 49546

Structural/Mechanical/Electrical Engineer
Greiner, Inc.
Grand Rapids, Michigan

Contractor
Owen-Ames-Kimball Company
Grand Rapids, Michigan

Photographer
Gary Quesada, Korab/
Hedrich-Blessing
Troy, Michigan

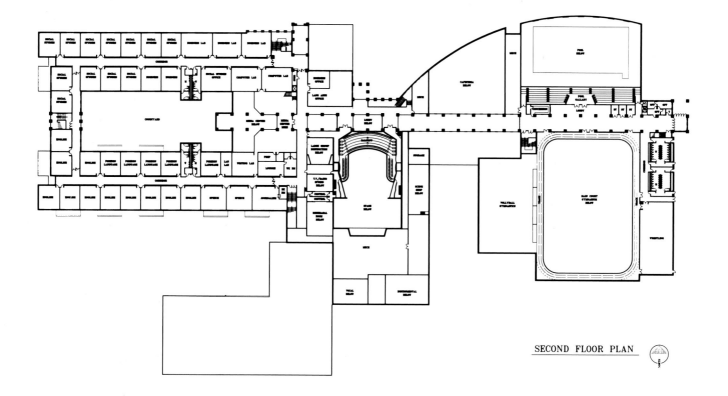

SECOND FLOOR PLAN

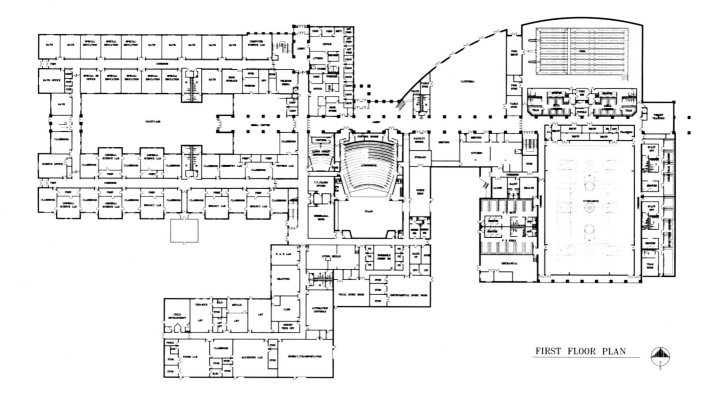

FIRST FLOOR PLAN

Seneca Valley Senior High School

Harmony, Pennsylvania

ARCHITECT'S STATEMENT

The facility is designed to be economical to construct and maintain. Because the new facility sits on the same 188-acre site as the existing high school, the design was required to make no unnecessary duplication of facilities, such as a full-size auditorium, pool, and boiler plant. In addition to addressing these isssues, the design team focused on environmental and energy concerns and on emerging technology for information distribution throughout the building

Honoring a request from the district that the school reflect and promote a community atmosphere throughout Seneca Valley, students in each community are designing flaygs that will be displayed in the lobby.

Owner
Seneca Valley School District

Data

Type of Facility
High school

Type of Construction
New

Area of Building
191,980 GSF

Cost of Construction
$17,303,920

Cost of Educational Equipment
$2,529,377

Status of Project
Completed August 1994

Credits

Architect
Foreman Bashford Architects
Engineers, Inc.
525 West New Castle Street
Zelienople, Pennsylvania 16063

*Structural/Mechanical/Electrical
Engineers*
Foreman Bashford Architects
Engineers, Inc.
Zelienople, Pennsylvania

Contractor
Mascaro, Inc.
Pittsburgh, Pennsylvania

Photographer
Kevin Cooke, Graule Studios
Rochester, Pennsylvania

ZELIENOPLE

SEVEN FIELDS

LANCASTER

JACKSON

HARMONY

High Schools

South Western Senior High School

Hanover, Pennsylvania

ARCHITECT'S STATEMENT

The project shares a 100-acre rural site with the intermediate school. As the centerpiece of the campus, this major renovation project took over three years to complete without disrupting the educational curriculum.

The cornerstone of the project is the 2,000-seat fieldhouse with bowstring trussed roof. All mechanical equipment for this air-conditioned space is enclosed within an integrated appendage leaving the curved roof without penetration. Both the new auditorium and gymnasium occupy anchor positions along the front of the 600-foot-long main facade. A continuous glass arcade provides passage along the entire public realm of the building.

Owner
South Western School District

Data
Type of Facility
High school

Type of Construction
Renovation

Area of Building
246,041 GSF (104,900 new,
141,141 renovation)

Cost of Construction
$16,937,051 ($8,246,058 new,
$8,690,993 renovation)

Cost of Educational Equipment
$593,675

Status of Project
Completed December 1994

Credits
Architect
Hayes Large Architects
Logan Boulevard and Fifth Avenue,
P.O. Box 1784
Altoona, Pennsylvania 16603

Structural Engineer
Hayes Large Architects
Altoona, Pennsylvania

Mechanical/Electrical Engineer
Brinjac, Kambic, and Associates, Inc.
Harrisburg, Pennsylvania

Food Facilities Planning
Hammer Design Associates
Pittsburgh, Pennsylvania

Theater Consultant
Assembly Places International
Philadelphia, Pennsylvania

Contractor
E.E. Murray Construction Company
Lancaster, Pennsylvania

Photographer
Christopher Barone
Kingston, Pennsylvania

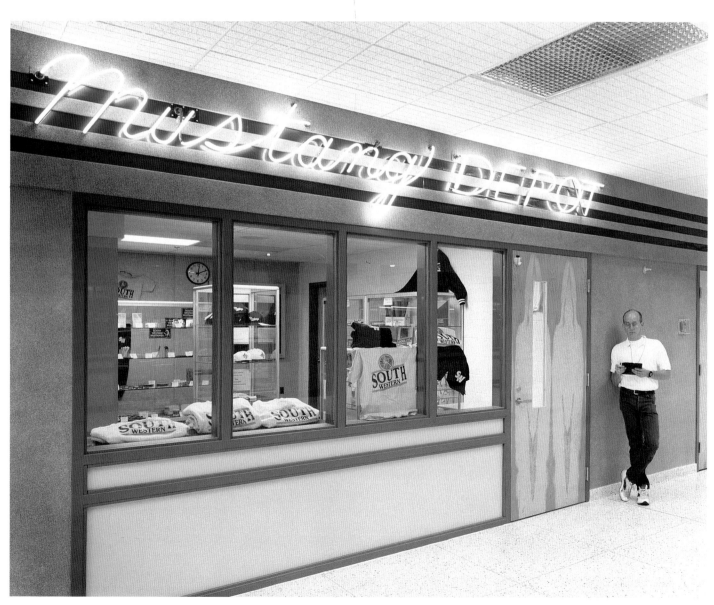

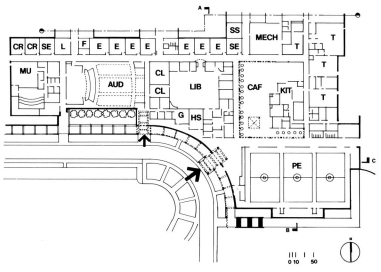

FIRST FLOOR

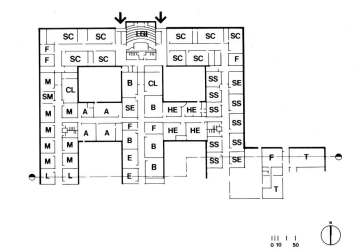

FIRST FLOOR

KEY

A	ART	M	MATHEMATICS
AD	ADMINISTRATION	MU	MUSIC SUITE
AG	ADAPTIVE GYM	SC	SCIENCE
B	BUSINESS	SE	SPECIAL EDUCATION
CL	COMPUTER LAB	SM	SEMINAR
E	ENGLISH	SS	SOCIAL STUDIES
F	FACULTY	T	TECHNICAL EDUCATION
G	GUIDANCE	TR	TEAM ROOM
H	HEALTH	WR	WEIGHT ROOM
HE	HOME ECONOMICS	LK	LOCKER ROOM
HS	HEALTH SUITE	TN	TRAINING ROOM
L	LANGUAGE	CR	GENERAL CLASSROOM

Warren Central High School

Indianapolis, Indiana

This project was undertaken to accommodate the addition of the ninth grade and to respond to changing curricula. The new north entrance delivers students and visitors to the commons. The commons is the circulation hub that is both a gathering space and a crossroads for primary corridors. The media center is accessible from the commons and is a large, naturally illuminated space that has the flexibility to accommodate current and future educational technology. The cafeteria is also accessed from the commons and can be subdivided via an operable wall. Corridors and vertical circulation have been enhanced to improve student movement and public access.

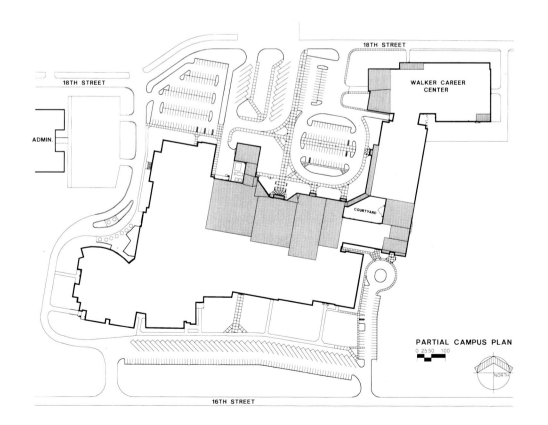

PARTIAL CAMPUS PLAN

0 25 50 100

NORTH

Owner
M.S.D. of Warren Township

Data

Type of Facility
High school

Type of Construction
Combined (17 percent new,
83 percent renovation)

Area of Building
725,000 GSF (125,000 new,
600,000 renovation)

Cost of Construction
$26,121,915 ($11,363,033 new,
$14,758,882 renovation)

Cost of Educational Equipment
$1,366,374

Status of Project
Completed February 1995

Credits

Architect
Fanning/Howey Associates, Inc.
3750 Priority Way Drive, Suite 110
Indianapolis, Indiana 46240

*Structural/Mechanical/Electrical
Engineer*
Fanning/Howey Associates, Inc.
Indianapolis, Indiana

Food Services Consultant
Vorndran Associates, Inc.
Fort Wayne, Indiana

Construction Manager
Toth-Ervin, Inc.
Indianapolis, Indiana

Photographer
Emery Photography
Columbus, Ohio

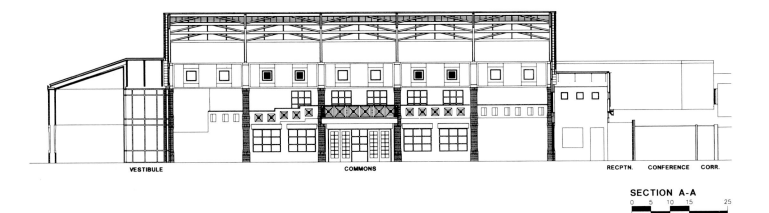

VESTIBULE   COMMONS   RECPTN.   CONFERENCE   CORR.

SECTION A-A

0   5   10   15   25

High Schools

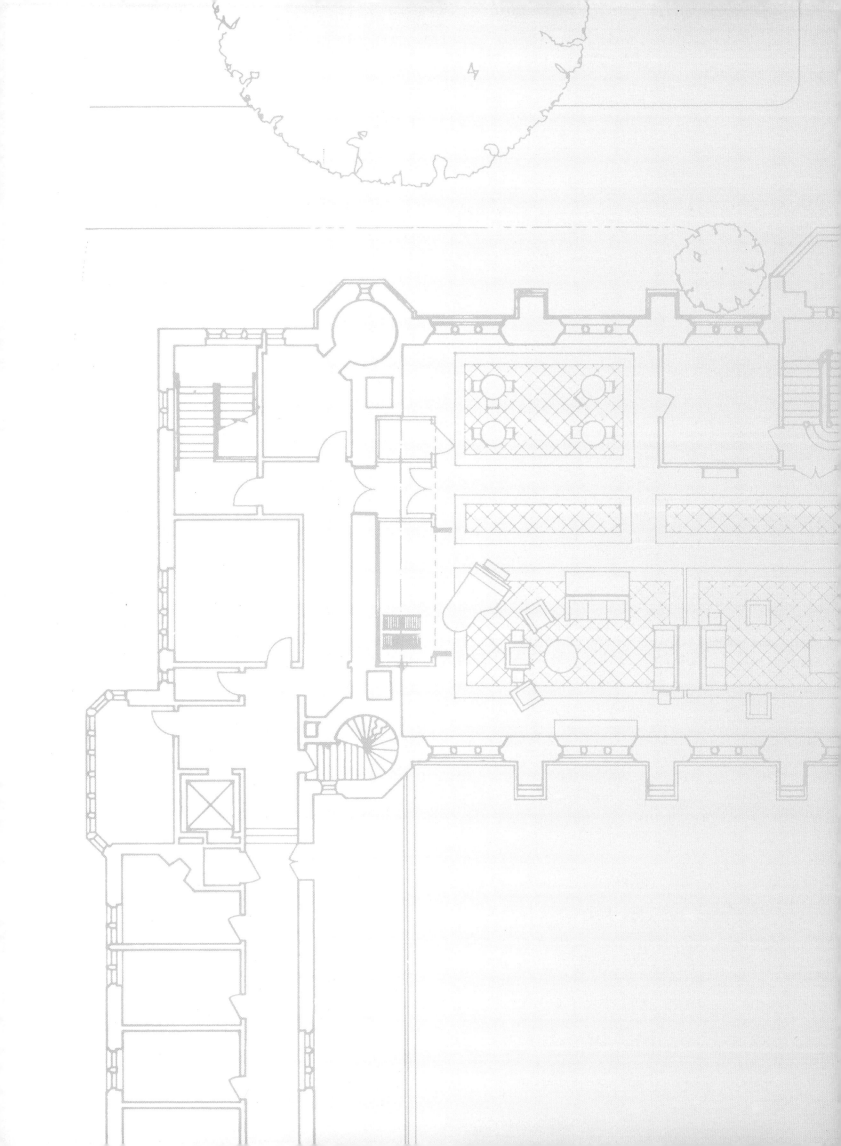

Multiuse Facilities

New Dining Hall and Student Center Renovations
Springside School

Philadelphia, Pennsylvania

ARCHITECT'S STATEMENT

The project includes new dining facilities for 300 people at a private girls' school, with distinct eating areas, one room for meetings, and outdoor dining. The renovated circulation spine called "Main Street" incorporates gallery space, a study area, and a lounge.

Special features include passive cooling and heating accomplished by the siting of a pavilion and the use of pergola to support climbing vines for natural shade, bringing in natural light through windows and a light monitor, while keeping new square footage minimal to follow budgetary and maintenance cost constraints. The appeal of the renovated space has caused a dramatic increase in new enrollment and greater use of space well beyond the original functions needed by the client.

Owner
    The Springside School

Data
    Type of Facility
        Multiple use: dining hall and
        student center

    Type of Construction
        Combined (17 percent new,
        83 percent renovated)

    Area of Building
        13,797 GSF (2,346 new,
        11,451 renovated)

    Cost of Construction
        $972,000

    Cost of Educational Equipment
        $62,000

    Status of Project
        Completed September 1994

Credits
    Architect
        Voith & Mactavish Architects
        1616 Walnut Street, 24th Floor
        Philadelphia, Pennsylvania
        19103-5397

    Structural Engineer
        O'Donnell & Naccarato
        Philadelphia, Pennsylvania

    Mechanical/Electrical Engineer
        Schiller & Hersh
        Oreland, Pennsylvania

    Food Service Consultant
        Ivan Bass
        Bensalem, Pennsylvania

    Contractor
        E. Allen Reeves, Inc.
        Abington, Pennsylvania

    Photographers
        (Color)
        Tom Bernard
        Berwyn, Pennsylvania

        (Black and White)
        Nick Kelsh
        Philadelphia, Pennsylvania

SOUTH ELEVATION

SECTION

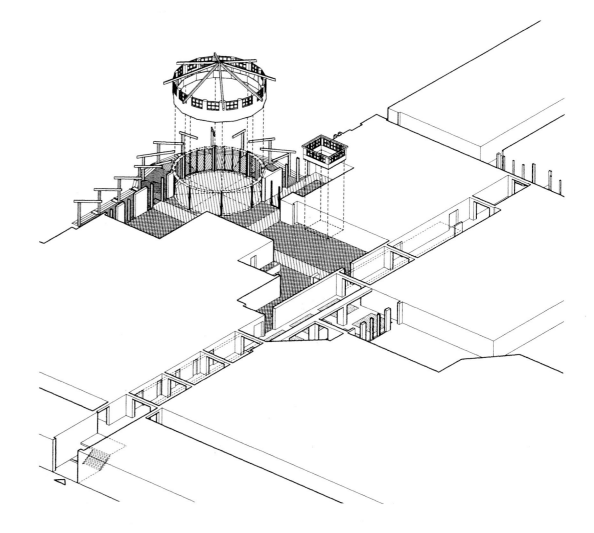

Renovation and Restoration of Thomas Great Hall
Bryn Mawr College

Bryn Mawr, Pennsylvania

ARCHITECT'S STATEMENT

The project involved the restoration and renovation of Thomas Library, designed by Cope & Stewardson in 1903. Interiors and lighting were designed to complement the restoration work. The building received National Historic Landmark status based on the importance of the Collegiate Gothic architectural style and the role that Ms. M. Carey Thomas played in women's education. The space is used for dinners, dances, and performances (lectures, readings, music, and small theatricals) and serves as lounge, study and reception space. Easy configuration changes were made possible by furniture design and a new storage unit in the back room.

Owner
Bryn Mawr College

Data

Type of Facility
Multiple use: performance

Type of Construction
Renovation

Area of Building
6,000 GSF

Cost of Construction
$725,000

Cost of Educational Equipment
$30,000

Status of Project
Completed September 1992

Credits

Architect
Voith & Mactavish Architects
1616 Walnut Street, 24th Floor
Philadelphia, Pennsylvania
19103-5397

Structural Engineers
Keast & Hood Company
Philadelphia, Pennsylvania

Gredell & Associates, Inc.
Wilmington, Delaware

Mechanical/Electrical Engineer
Dimitri J. Ververelli, Inc.
Consulting Engineers
Philadelphia, Pennsylvania

Lighting Consultants
Tigue Lighting
Philadelphia, Pennsylvania

Historical Consultants
Clio Group
(firm now defunct)

Contractor
Haverstick-Borthwick, Inc.
Plymouth Meeting, Pennsylvania

Photographer
Tom Bernard
Berwyn, Pennsylvania

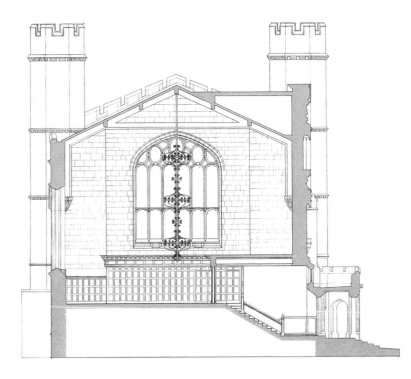

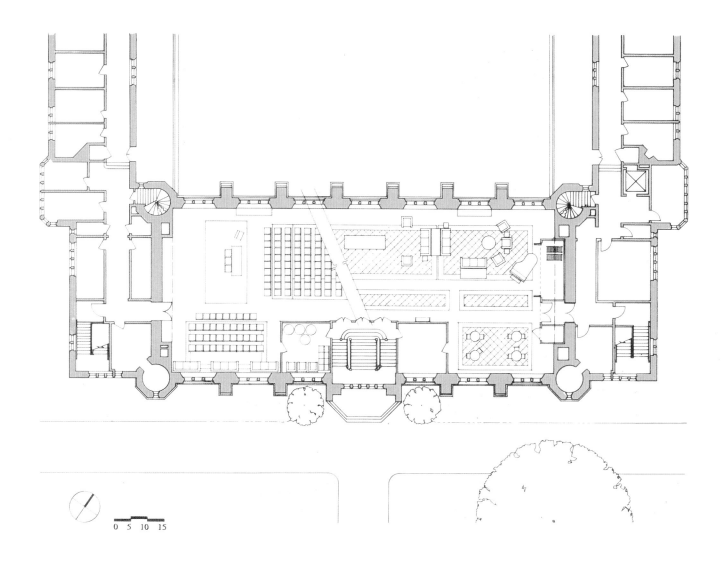

0 5 10 15

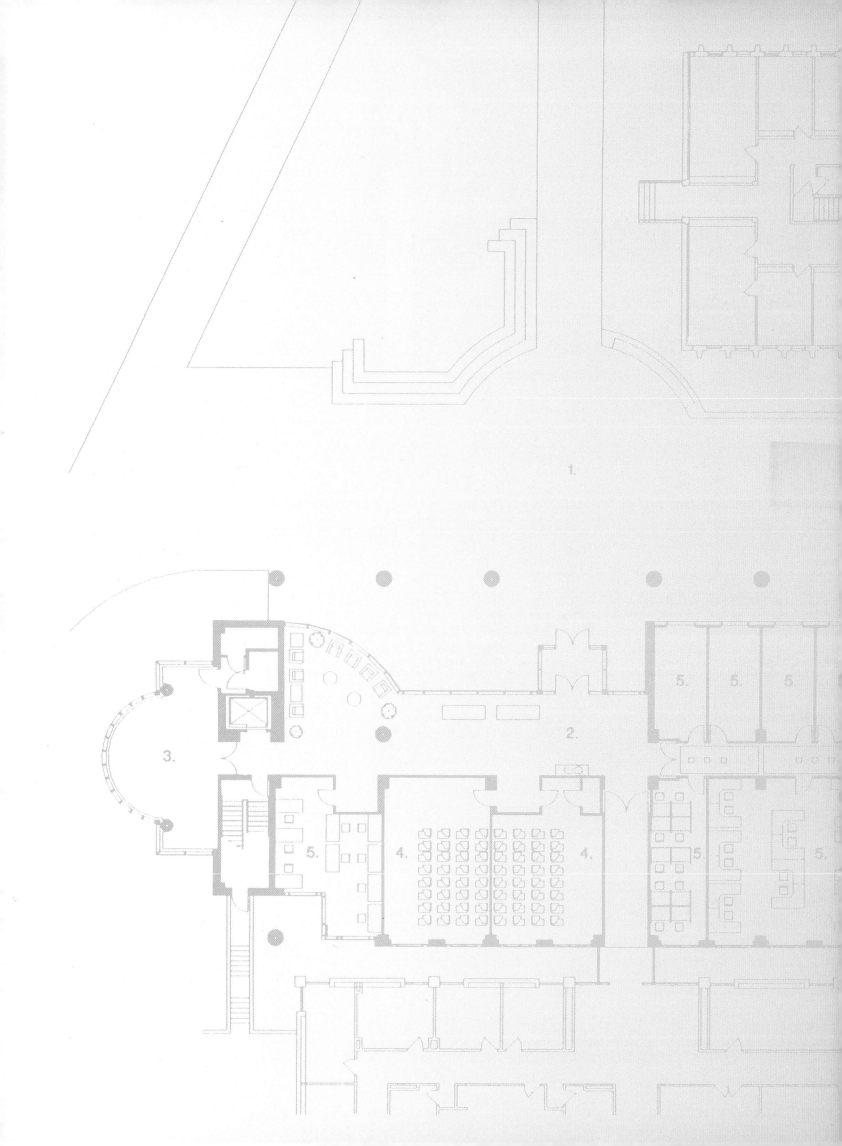

Universities

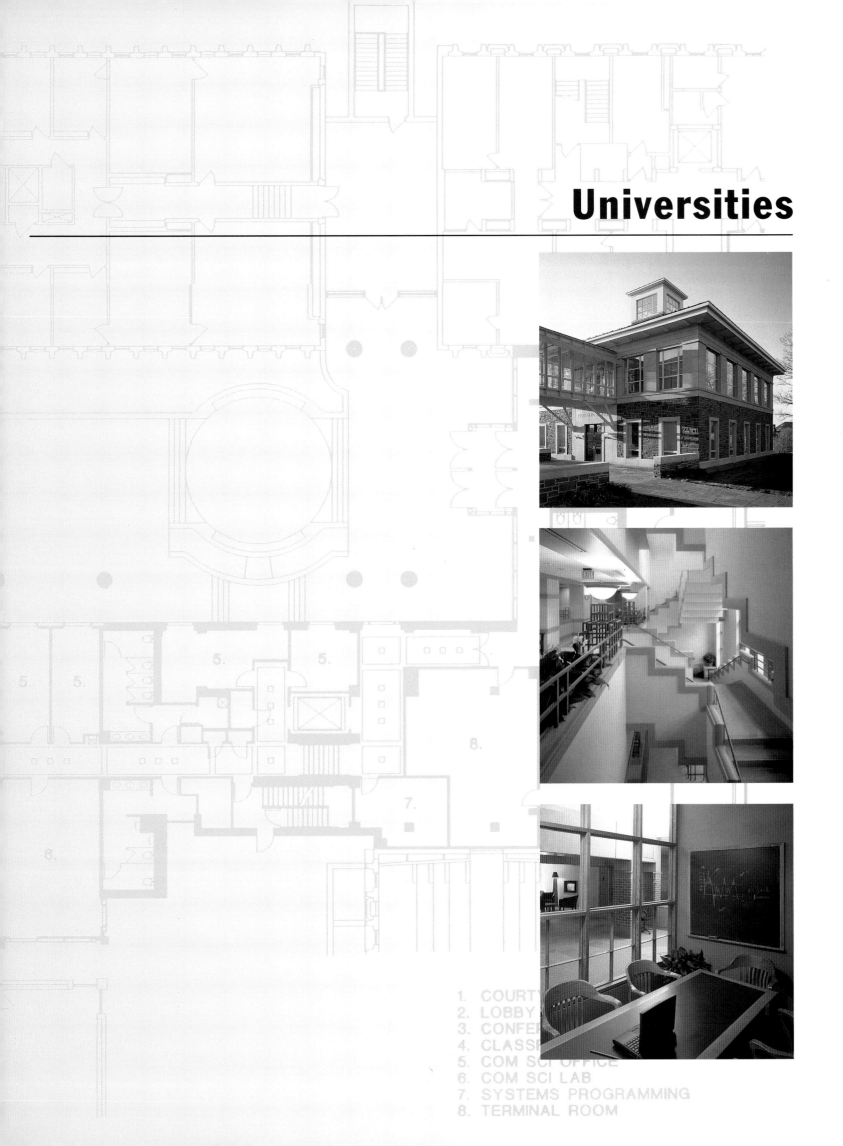

1. COURTY...
2. LOBBY
3. CONFE...
4. CLASS...
5. COM SCI OFFICE
6. COM SCI LAB
7. SYSTEMS PROGRAMMING
8. TERMINAL ROOM

Business School and Mass Communications Center
Quinnipiac College

Hamden, Connecticut

Citation

The gateway of this high-technology business and media center establishes its identity with a glass dome and maximum use of lighting. The new center ties the campus together, yet it shapes its own space on the site, suggesting formality without being unfriendly. The well-detailed interior offers a fresh approach to Modernism, with televisions used as decor, discussion areas outside each classroom area, and dramatic lighting.

Owner
   Quinnipiac College

Data
   Type of Facility
      Academic Business School

   Type of Construction
      New

   Area of Building
      43,550 GSF

   Cost of Construction
      $6,538,356

   Cost of Education Equipment
      $1,200,000

   Status of Project
      Completed September 1994

Credits
   Architect
      Centerbrook, Architects and
      Planners
      P.O. Box 955
      Essex, Connecticut 06426

   Structural Engineer
      Besier Gibble Norden, Consulting
      Engineers
      Old Saybrook, Connecticut

   Mechanical/Electrical Engineer
      J.E. Berning, Consulting Engineer
      (deceased)

   Contractor
      F. I. P. Construction, Inc.
      Cheshire, Connecticut

   Photographer
      Jeff Goldberg, Esto Photographics
      Mamaroneck, New York

ARCHITECT'S STATEMENT

This new building forms the northern boundary of the central quadrangle of a small college in New England. The building is divided into two wings, separated by an arched portal which provides a ceremonial gateway into the quadrangle from the main parking areas to the north.

The various functions within the building are arranged along a distinctive path that passes under the dome and extends inside both wings of the building. In the classroom wing, several lounges on the edge of the path encourage spontaneous gatherings and conversation. Small team study rooms share daylight from the clerestory windows, bringing sunshine into the inner part of the building. Three case-method lecture halls, with seating in the round, take the focus away from the teacher and encourage interaction among the students in simulation of real life business dealings. Televisions positioned at the head of each column supporting the clerestory window wall broadcast the latest news and world market reports.

In the mass communications wing, the hallway, again edged with small lounges, passes by the windowed radio studio and terminates at a circular lounge which allows visitors and interested students to view the control room and television studios beyond.

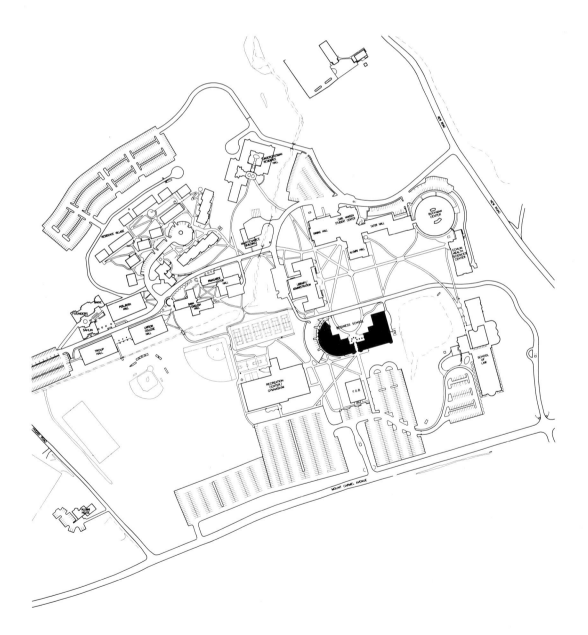

SITE

0 50 100 200

Volen National Center for Complex Systems
Brandeis University

Waltham, Massachusetts

Citation

Both the research and administrative spaces are well-defined in this facility, with student and faculty offices that are organized to facilitate interaction. Exterior site development—entries, piazzas, and other gathering places—extend this interaction beyond the building walls. The support system for the building is incorporated into the aesthetic design to create an environment that relates well to its purpose as an engineering research center; for example, structural materials such as concrete are left exposed. The project reflects much consideration for balancing and harmonizing its elements.

Owner
Brandeis University

Data

Type of Facility
Interdisciplinary research center

Type of Construction
New

Area of Building
55,000 GSF

Cost of Construction
$11,000,000

Status of Project
Phase I completed May 1994

Credits

Architect
Cannon
One Center Plaza
Boston, Massachusetts 02108

Structural Engineer
Boston Building Consultants
Boston, Massachusetts

Mechanical/Electrical Engineer
Cannon
Grand Island, New York

Laboratory Consultant
Earl Walls Associates
San Diego, California

Landscape Design
Pressley Associates Inc.
Cambridge, Massachusetts

Acoustical/Vibration/Shielding Consultant
Acentech Incorporated
Cambridge, Massachusetts

Contractor
Walsh Brothers, Inc.
Waltham, Massachusetts

Photographer
Richard Mandelkorn
Lincoln, Massachusetts

ARCHITECT'S STATEMENT

This national energy center combines programs of computer science and artificial intelligence, cognitive science and perception, neuroscience and structural biology. The mission of this center for excellence is to develop programs such as complex system modeling, neural networks, parallel computers, and advanced energy technologies. With special focus on interdisciplinary sciences, the building supports and encourages sharing of facilities and information. The location of departments reflects the relationship of their disciplines. For example, experimental and perceptual psychology is adjacent to the neuroscience department and the existing biology building, while linguistics and cognitive science are next to computer science.

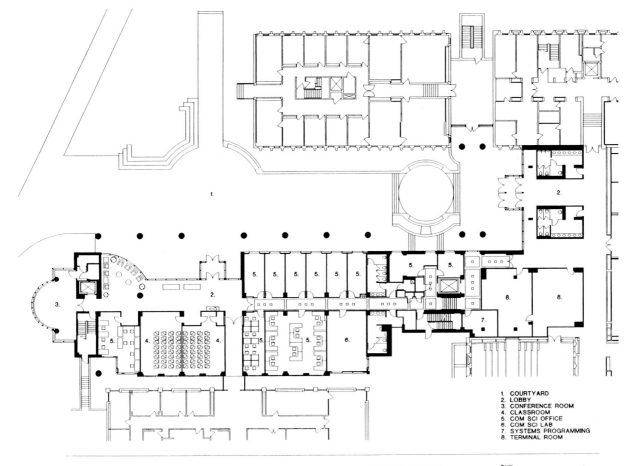

1. COURTYARD
2. LOBBY
3. CONFERENCE ROOM
4. CLASSROOM
5. COM SCI OFFICE
6. COM SCI LAB
7. SYSTEMS PROGRAMMING
8. TERMINAL ROOM

GROUND FLOOR

Scale
0   5   10   20

N ◯

Engineering Building at the Naval Postgraduate School

San Bruno, California

ARCHITECT'S STATEMENT

There were a number of challenges associated with the Engineering and Classroom Building at the Naval Postgraduate School. In order to accommodate the 50 different research and testing laboratories and provide a controlled academic environment, the facility includes three individual structures. A two-story structure housing the industrial labs is connected by an entry lobby to a smaller three-story building accommodating classrooms and offices. The third structure is a physically separated, octagonally shaped lecture hall. The building blends harmoniously with the school's existing International style of architecture and sits prominently at the entry to the campus.

WEST ELEVATION

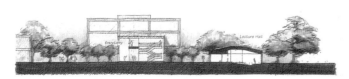

SECTION THROUGH ENTRY LOBBY

Owner
United States Navy

Data

Type of Facility
Laboratory and classroom building

Type of Construction
New

Area of Building
67,000 GSF

Cost of Construction
$9,400,000

Cost of Educational Equipment
$2,000,000

Status of Project
Completed April 1995

Credits

Architect
Crosby Helmich Architects
33 New Montgomery Street,
Suite 950
San Francisco, California

Design Architect
Gary R. Frye
1624 Tiburon Boulevard
Tiburon, California 94920

Structural Engineer
DASSE Design
San Francisco, California

Mechanical/Electrical Engineer
Buonaccorsi & Associates
San Francisco, California

Civil Engineer
Creegan & D'Angelo
Monterey, California

Landscape Architect
Eldon Beck Associates
San Rafael, California

Contractor
Alan Bender
West Sacramento, California

Photographer
Donna Kempner
San Francisco, California

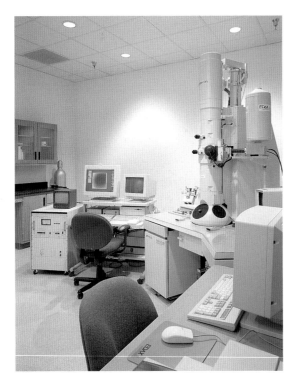

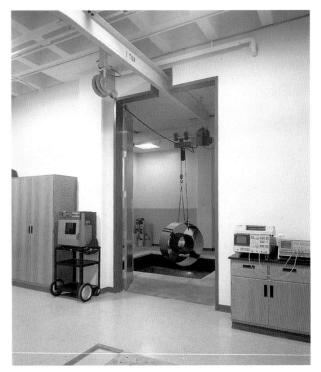

Pappajohn Business Administration Building
University of Iowa

Iowa City, Iowa

ARCHITECT'S STATEMENT

The architects took their cues for the design from the century-old limestone buildings of the Pentacrest in the heart of the central campus. Rising four stories and occupying most of a city block, the scale and feeling of the exterior reflect the grace and serene neo-classicism of the nearby structures. The "L"-shaped building produces a landscaped court in the center of the site, which serves to extend the open spaces formed by the Pentacrest. This creates a private out-door courtyard for the school, while efficiently utilizing the limited land resources to achieve the maximum building square footage. The building extends the classroom itself, with state-of-the-art technology that literally connects students to the world. This technology, found in every classroom and auditorium, has revolutionized the teaching process of the College of Business Administration.

Owner
University of Iowa

Data

Type of Facility
Undergraduate and Graduate
College of Business Administration

Type of Construction
New

Area of Building
169,300 GSF

Cost of Construction
$22,000,000

Cost of Educational Equipment
$3,500,000

Status of Project
Completed January 1994

Credits

Architect
Neumann Monson P.C.
111 East College Street
Iowa City, Iowa 52240

Design Architect
Architectural Resources Cambridge
140 Mt. Auburn Street
Cambridge, Massachusetts 02138

Structural Engineer
Jack Miller & Associates
Cedar Rapids, Iowa

Mechanical/Electrical Engineer
Alvine & Associates, Inc.
Omaha, Nebraska

Lighting Consultant
LAM Partners, Inc.
Cambridge, Massachusetts

Acoustics & Vibration Consultant
L.G. Copley Associates
Needham, Massachusetts

Construction Cost Estimating
Stecker-Harmsen, Inc.
Ames, Iowa

Contractor
Mid America Construction Company
Iowa City, Iowa

Photographer
Wheeler Photographics
Weston, Massachusetts

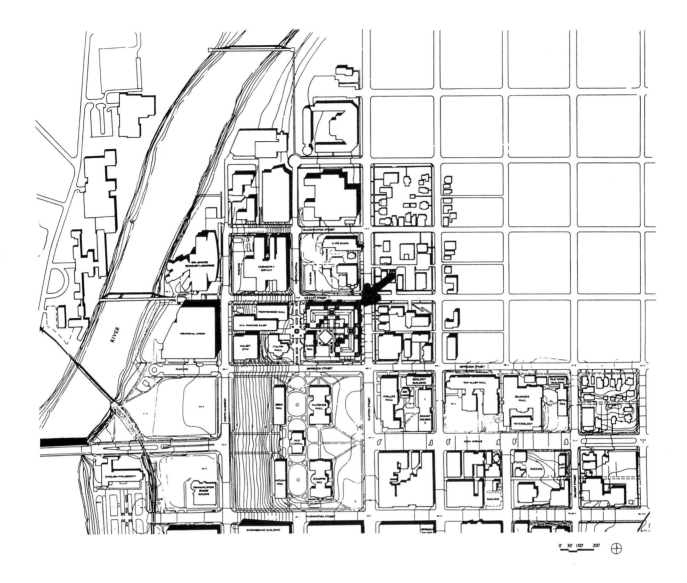

Persson Hall
Colgate University

Hamilton, New York

This 36,800-square-foot academic building creates a physical link between the upper and lower areas of Colgate's campus. At the convergence of two major pedestrian paths leading up the hill, Persson Hall forms a gateway in both directions. Together with the existing library, student union, and arts complex below it, the building contributes to the development of a new center of student activities. The two volumes of the building are connected below ground by a lobby and at the second level by a transparent bridge. The glass-enclosed bridge functions as an informal meeting place and offers dramatic views of both the distinguished upper campus buildings and the vista of the lake below.

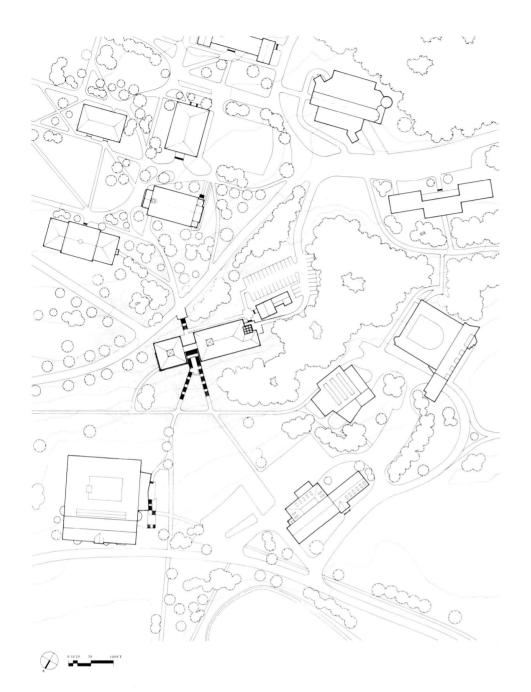

Owner
Colgate University

Data

Type of Facility
Classrooms and office space for
university departments

Type of Construction
New

Area of Building
36,800 GSF

Cost of Construction
$5,500,000

Cost of Educational Equipment
$414,500

Status of Project
Completed September 1994

Credits

Architect
Tai Soo Kim Partners
285 Farmington Avenue
Hartford, Connecticut 06105

Structural Engineer
Klepper, Hahn & Hyatt
East Syracuse, New York

Mechanical/Electrical Engineer
Fraser & Fassler
Syracuse, New York

Landscape Architects
Rolland/Towers
New Haven, Connecticut

Cost Estimators
Andrew Cartwell & Company
Boston, Massachusetts

Contractor
J.D. Taylor Construction Company
Syracuse, New York

Photographer
Nick Wheeler
Wheeler Photographics
Weston, Massachusetts

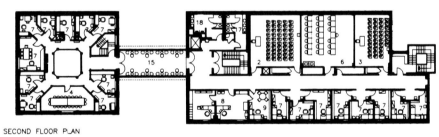

SECOND FLOOR PLAN

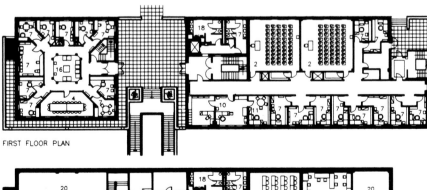

FIRST FLOOR PLAN

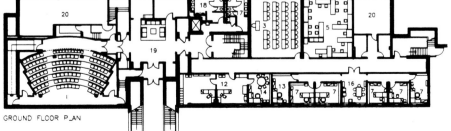

GROUND FLOOR PLAN

1 AUDITORIUM
   115 SEATS
2 CLASSROOM
   50 SEATS
3 CLASSROOM
   35 SEATS
4 CLASSROOM
   20 SEATS
5 CARTOGRAPHY LAB
6 COMPUTER LAB
7 FACULTY OFFICES
8 ECONOMICS DEPT
   OFFICE
9 ECONOMICS CHAIRMAN
10 POL. SCI. DEPT
   OFFICE
11 POL. SCI. CHAIRMAN
12 GEOGRAPHY DEPT
   OFFICE
13 GEOGRAPHY CHAIRMAN
14 DIVISION DIRECTOR
15 STUDENT LOUNGE
16 FACULTY LOUNGE
17 MEN'S RESTROOMS
18 WOMEN'S RESTROOMS
19 LOBBY
20 MECH & ELEC

0 4' 8' 16'

Shapiro Admissions Center
Brandeis University

Waltham, Massachusetts

A R C H I T E C T ' S S T A T E M E N T

The building was originally designed in the 1950s as a plain-looking commuter student retreat near the campus entry. Prior to this renovation, admissions offices were hidden on the third floor of a building at the school's farthest reaches. The university engaged in this project to move the admissions office to a highly visible, inviting, and readily accessible facility.

The new design recharges the modernist campus's emotional impact for visitors. It contains the entire Admissions Department, including a large reception room, a presentation hall, conference rooms, 14 interview offices, a processing/clerical center, and other amenities.

O w n e r
Brandeis University

D a t a
Type of Facility
University admissions office

Type of Construction
Renovation

Area of Building
10,000 GSF

Cost of Construction
$1,400,000

Cost of Furniture
$200,000

Status of Project
Competed September 1994

C r e d i t s
Architect
Centerbrook, Architects and
Planners
P.O. Box 955
Essex, Connecticut 06426

Structural Engineer
Besier Gibble Norden, Consulting
Engineers, Inc.
Old Saybrook, Connecticut

Mechanical/Electrical Engineer
Robert Van Houten
Essex, Connecticut

Landscape Architect
Morgan Wheelock
Boston, Massachusetts

Contractor
Brandeis University/Twilight
Construction
Newton, Massachusetts

Photographer
Steve Rosenthal
Auburndale, Massachusetts

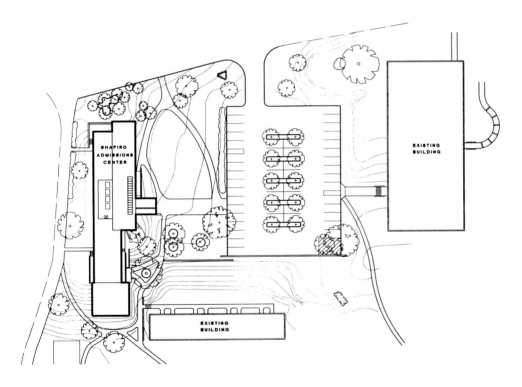

SITE PLAN

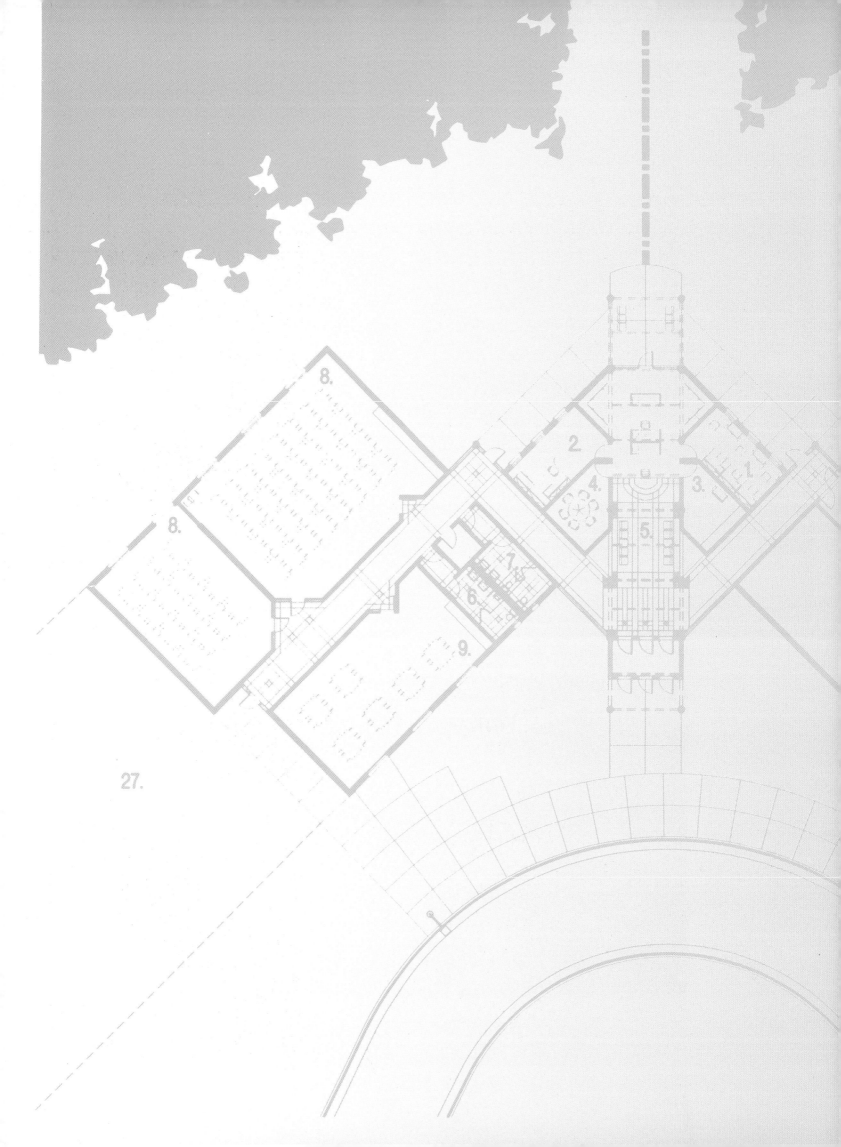

Other Projects

Aircraft Rescue and Fire Fighting Training Facility (ARFFT)

Duluth, Minnesota

ARCHITECT'S STATEMENT

The Aircraft Rescue and Fire Fighting Training Facility (ARFFT) provides training for career and military fire fighters, fire fighting students and airport personnel. Training exercises are run from the classroom building, which serves as a remote fire hall, education center, equipment decontamination and maintenance facility, and administration building. The simulator utilizes state-of-the-art technology to create environmentally safe, mock fires with the same intensity and smoke density produced by jet fuel fires. An operator controls all fire scenarios from a terminal in the control tower overlooking the simulator. An on-site water treatment plant treats all of the runoff from the simulator exercises.

Owner
  Lake Superior College

Data
  Type of Facility
    Training

  Type of Construction
    New

  Area of Building
    34,246 GSF

  Cost of Construction
    $5,269,667

  Cost of Educational Equipment
    $4,824,132

  Status of Project
    Completed May 1994

Credits
  Architect
    The Stanius Johnson Architects, Inc.
    1831 East Eighth Street
    Duluth, Minnesota 55812

    in association with
    Contraves U.S.A.
    5902 Breckenridge Parkway
    Tampa, Florida 33610

  Structural Engineer
    Krech & Ojard Consulting
    Duluth, Minnesota

  Mechanical/Electrical Engineer
    Foster, Jacobs and Johnson, Inc.
    Duluth, Minnesota

  Civil Engineer
    RREM, Inc.
    Duluth, Minnesota

  Contractor
    Reuben Johnson & Son, Inc.
    Superior, Wisconsin

  Photographer
    Don F. Wong Photography
    Minneapolis, Minnesota

    Jeff Frey & Associates
    Duluth, Minnesota

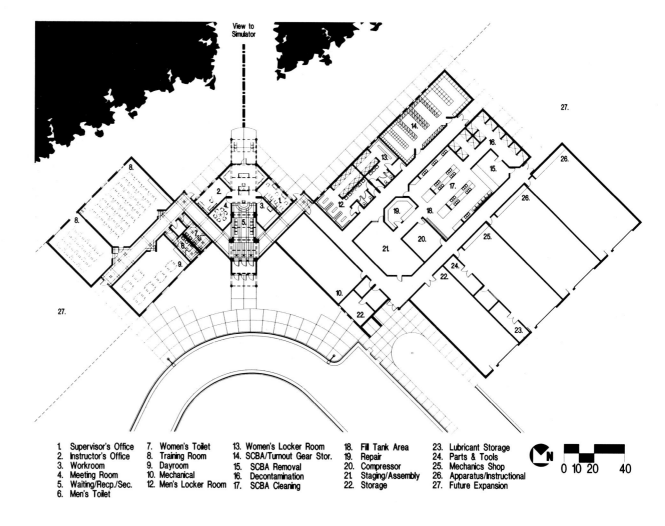

1.	Supervisor's Office	7.	Women's Toilet	13.	Women's Locker Room	18.	Fill Tank Area	23.	Lubricant Storage
2.	Instructor's Office	8.	Training Room	14.	SCBA/Turnout Gear Stor.	19.	Repair	24.	Parts & Tools
3.	Workroom	9.	Dayroom	15.	SCBA Removal	20.	Compressor	25.	Mechanics Shop
4.	Meeting Room	10.	Mechanical	16.	Decontamination	21.	Staging/Assembly	26.	Apparatus/Instructional
5.	Waiting/Recp./Sec.	12.	Men's Locker Room	17.	SCBA Cleaning	22.	Storage	27.	Future Expansion
6.	Men's Toilet								

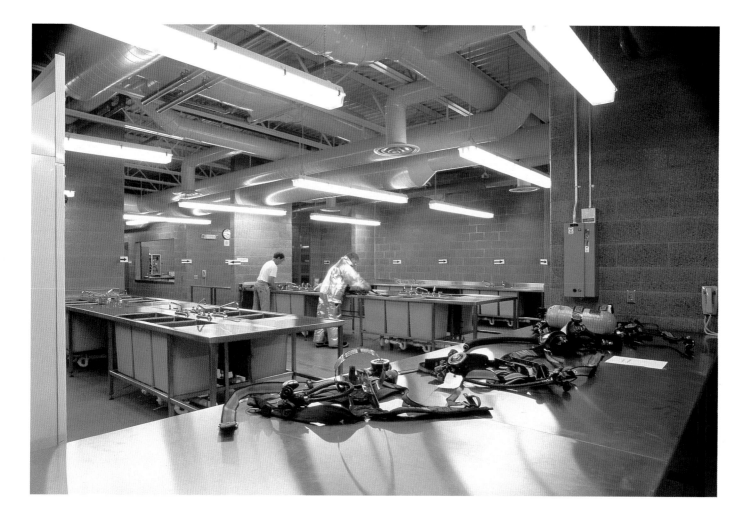

The Thomas and Dorothy Leavey Library
University of Southern California

Los Angeles, California

A R C H I T E C T ' S   S T A T E M E N T

This new facility has been developed as a gateway library, designed to integrate traditional information services with emerging educational and information technologies. In a new approach to traditional reference department functions, an 8,500-GSF Information Commons houses a core reference collection and offers computer consultation and research assistance. To facilitate student interaction, the Commons and adjacent spaces include a variety of learning/teaching spaces:

- Clusters providing 100 computing/multimedia workstations in configurations;

- Twenty-one collaborative study and teaching rooms;

- Two classrooms for training in library skills, database searching and use of Internet data resources; and

- A 50-seat, fully mediated auditorium.

The Center for Scholarly Technology—a unique resource for faculty as well as students—provides space for research, training in information access and manipulation, and analysis and curriculum development using newer technologies.

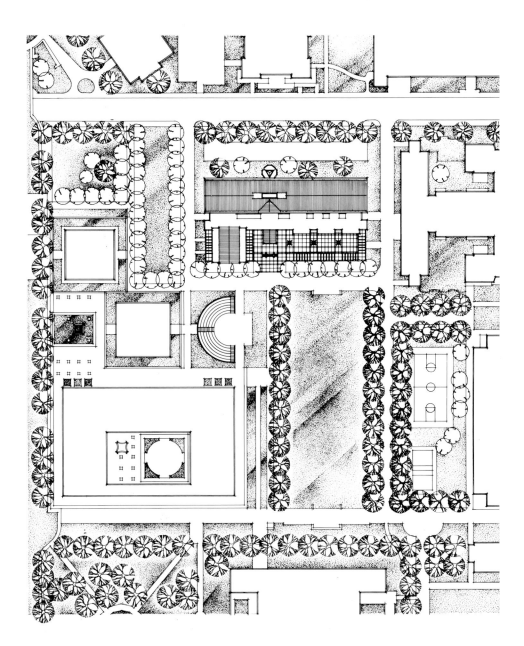

Owner
University of Southern California

Data

Type of Facility
Library

Type of Construction
New

Area of Building
94,000 GSF

Cost of Construction
$15,100,000

Cost of Furnishings and Educational Equipment
$2,300,000

Status of Project
Completed September 1994

Credits

Architect
Shepley Bulfinch Richardson and Abbott
40 Broad Street
Boston, Massachusetts 02109

Building Engineer
Ove Arup & Partners
Los Angeles, California

Landscape Consultant
Pamela Burton & Company
(formerly Burton & Spitz)
Santa Monica, California

Contractor
McCarthy Construction
Newport Beach, California

Photographer
Timothy Hursley
Little Rock, Arkansas

Living and Learning Center for Developmentally Disabled Adults

Olney, Maryland

ARCHITECT'S STATEMENT

The program, to create a living and learning center in a "normalized" noninstitutional environment, was achieved by a campus-like site plan and design subtleties—the curving alignment that creates a community of buildings, the arcade linking the residential buildings to each other, the low steel-columned front porch of the educational building, and powerful wooden trusses supporting the roof.

Designed in a contemporary vernacular style in response to surrounding farm structures, the educational building and residential buildings (on 10 acres) serve 40 clients and staff, as well as nine resident clients and their caretakers. Incorporating forms reminiscent of silos and barns, the educational building is sited perpendicular to the hillside to maximize the use of green space and features a northern wall of structural steel and glass—bringing in plentiful light and framing a spectacular view of the hills. The auditorium/gym is the primary interior space of the building, with all paths leading to it.

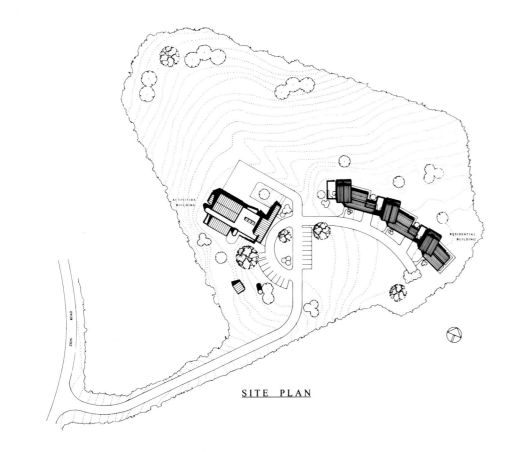

SITE PLAN

Owner

    American Foundation for Autistic Children

Data

Type of Facility

    Residential learning center

Type of Construction

    New

Area of Building

    13,400 GSF

Cost of Construction

    $1,200,000

Cost of Educational Equipment

    $100,000

Status of Project

    Completed May 1993

Credits

Architect

    Schick Goldstein Architects
    1506 19th Street, N.W.
    Washington, D.C. 20036

Structural Engineer

    Johns & Bhatia Engineering
    Consultants Ltd.
    Bethesda, Maryland

Mechanical/Electrical Engineer

    Shefferman & Bigelson Co.,
    Consulting Engineers
    Silver Spring, Maryland

Civil Engineer

    Macris Hendricks & Glascock
    Gaithersburg, Maryland

Lighting Design Consultant

    Conventry Lighting Associates
    Washington, D.C.

Geotechnical Engineering

    Schnabel Engineering Associates
    Bethesda, Maryland

Contractor

    E.A. Baker Company
    Takoma Park, Maryland

Photographer

    Hoachlander Photography Studios
    Washington, D.C.

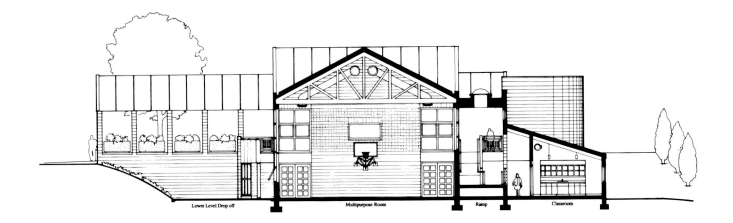

Lower Level Drop off   Multipurpose Room   Ramp   Classroom

SECTION

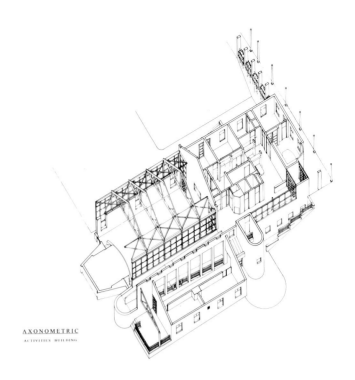

Addition and Renovation to Reed Library, State University of New York at Fredonia

Fredonia, New York

ARCHITECT'S STATEMENT

I.M. Pei's original Reed Library is integrally woven into his 1960s "heroic" central campus built entirely of a single buff concrete.

The four-story addition is attached to the south end of the existing single-floor structure. The addition makes the transition from the Pei campus center to the more traditional institutional brick buildings of the campus to the south. Its blank, curved concrete wall is the backdrop to the Pei building and defines the edge of the central campus. The addition's brick bar is cut by a three-story opening, axially connecting the south campus residential quarters to the existing entrance sequence of the original library building.

Owner
State University Construction Fund

Data
Type of Facility
Library

Type of Construction
Combined (36 percent new,
64 percent renovated)

Area of Building
117,500 GSF (42,500 GSF new,
75,000 GSF renovated)

Cost of Construction
$7,298,232 ($5,767,000 new,
$1,531,232 renovated)

Status of Project
Completed September 1994

Credits
Architect
Pasanella + Klein Stolzman + Berg
Architects, PC
330 West 42nd Street
New York, New York 10036

Structural Engineer
Siracuse Engineers
Buffalo, New York

Mechanical/Electrical Engineer
Babinsky-Klein Engineering
Amherst, New York

Library Design Consultant
Dr. Ellsworth Mason
Lexington, Kentucky

Lighting Design Consultant
Jerry Kugler Associates
New York, New York

Contractor
Phase I:
Whipple Allen Construction Company
Erie, Pennsylvania

Phase II:
L.G. Hall Building Contractor, Inc.
Amherst, New York

Photographer
Paul Warchol
New York, New York

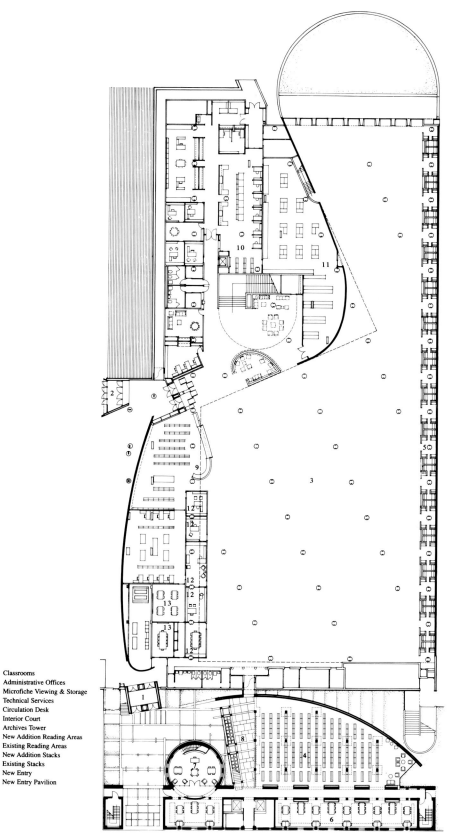

13. Classrooms
12. Administrative Offices
11. Microfiche Viewing & Storage
10. Technical Services
9. Circulation Desk
8. Interior Court
7. Archives Tower
6. New Addition Reading Areas
5. Existing Reading Areas
4. New Addition Stacks
3. Existing Stacks
2. New Entry
1. New Entry Pavilion

GROUND FLOOR

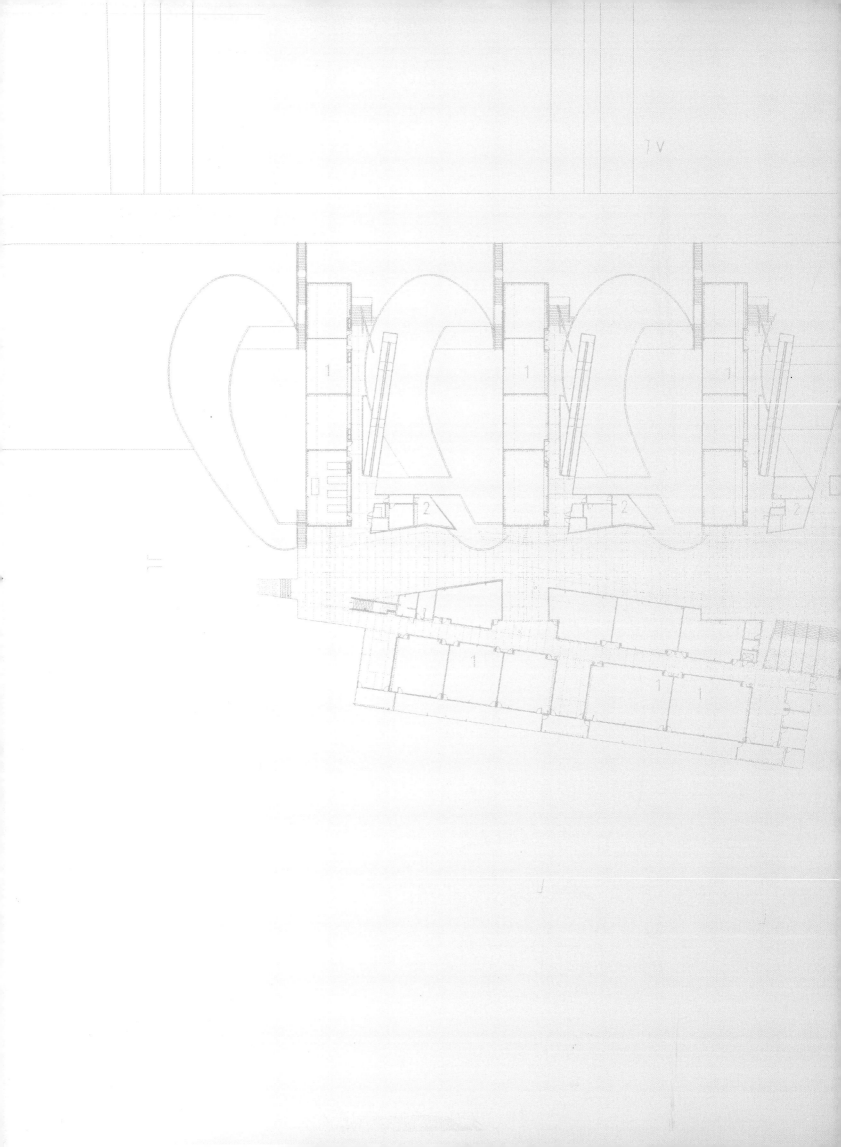

Epilogue

Diamond Ranch High School

Pomona, California

Offering a view to the future in both form and function, this California high school will truly be a school for the 21st century when it is completed. The architects have addressed three current issues: site environment, social groups, and educational flexibility. Clearly, the integration of this school into the landscape is a departure from the other buildings in this book: The school will not become an object but rather a part of the landscape. The design will encourage social groupings that extend beyond peer interaction to encompass faculty and administration, thus fostering a sense of collegiality. Educational flexibility in this case has a double meaning, providing individuals with the flexibility to pursue their interests and making the building flexible to accommodate future changes in technology.

This high school design seems to incorporate the best aspects of a "personal" education with the advantages of technology. This rare mix, which must become more common, is here embodied in an even rarer form that may be the future.

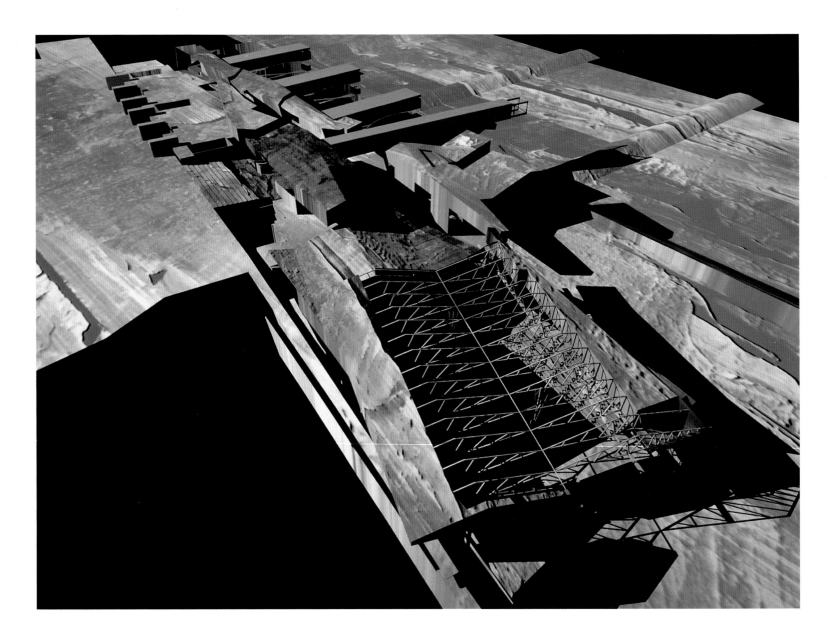

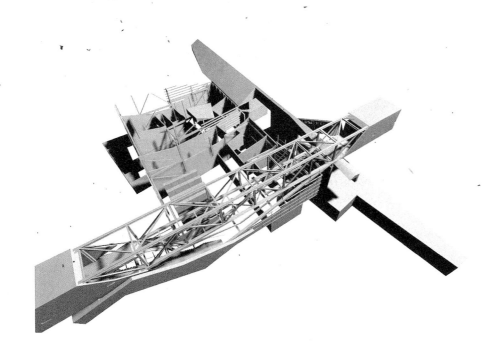

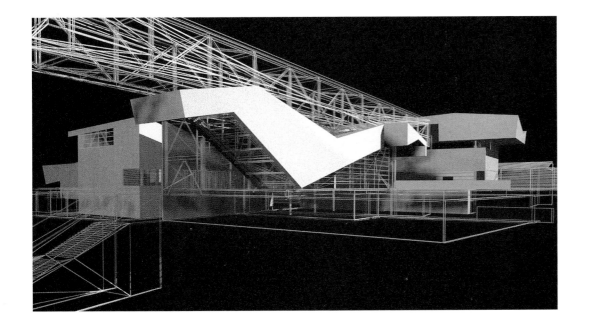

O w n e r
Pomona Unified School District

D a t a
Type of Facility
High school

Type of Construction
New

Area of Building
150,000 GSF

Cost of Construction
$20,000,000 (estimate)

Cost of Educational Equipment
$1,000,000 (estimate)

Status of Project
Estimated to be complete
September 1998

C r e d i t s
Architect
RTA/Blurock Architects, Inc.
1001 West 17th Street, #F
Costa Mesa, California 92627

Design Architect
Morphosis Architects
2041 Colorado Avenue
Santa Monica, California 90404

Structural/Mechanical/Electrical
Engineer
Ove Arup & Partners
Los Angeles, California

Civil Engineer
Andreasen Engineering, Inc.
Pomona, California

Landscape Architect
Fong & Associates
Costa Mesa, California

Contractor
Bidding in Summer of 1996

ARCHITECT'S STATEMENT

This project focuses on three major areas: the complex's conceptual stance toward the site environment, social groupings, and education flexibility. The first goal was to take advantage of the natural beauty of the site by integrating the play fields and buildings into the surrounding hillside. The second goal was to create a dynamic built environment that would foster maximum social interaction between students, teachers, administration, and the community. Finally, this project attempts to facilitate a flexible teaching environment that allows a solid foundation of core curriculum for grades nine through ten, and offers the opportunity for students to focus on specific program majors in grades eleven through twelve.

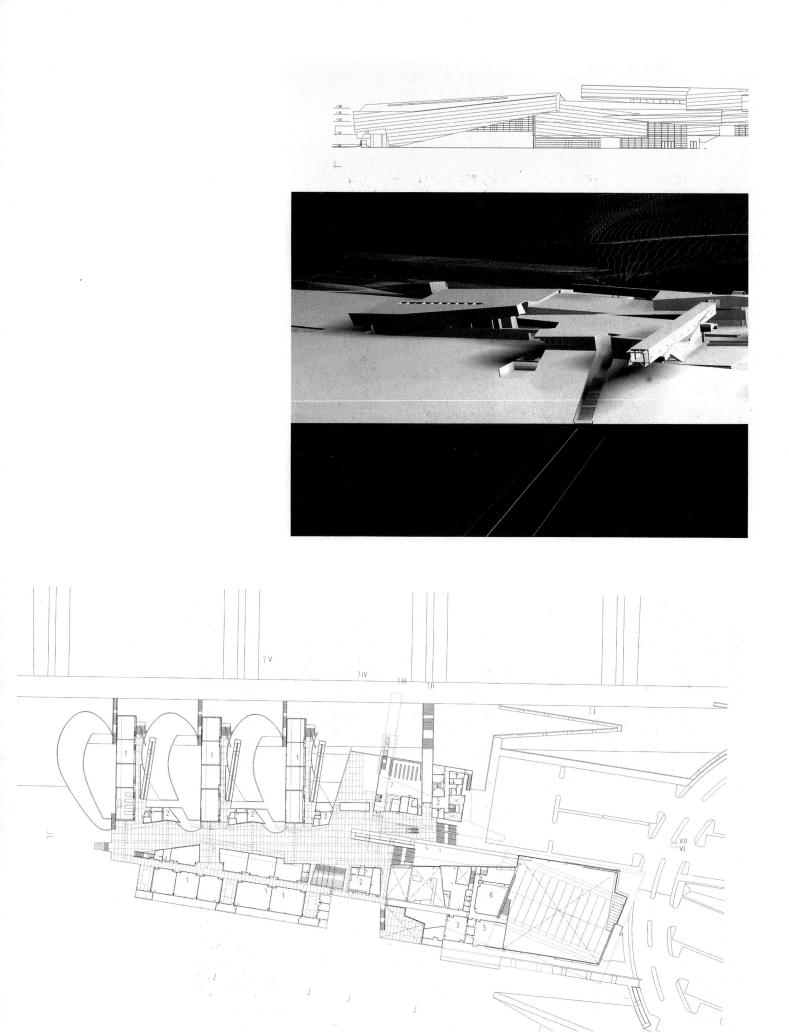

Index of Architects